Maharshi's Gospel

BOOKS I & II

Being Answers of
Bhagavan Sri Ramana Maharshi
to Questions Put to Him by Devotees

SRI RAMANASRAMAM
TIRUVANNAMALAI
INDIA

Sixteenth Edition	:	*2012*	—	*2000 copies*
Seventeenth Edition	:	*2016*	—	*2000 copies*
Eighteenth Edition	:	2020 (January)		

2000 copies

CC No: 1025

ISBN: 978-81-88018-02-4

Price: ₹ 35

Published by:
V.S. Ramanan
President
SRI RAMANASRAMAM
Tiruvannamalai 606 603
Tamil Nadu, INDIA
Web : www.sriramanamaharshi.org

Printed by:
Aaral Graphics
Chennai 600 094
Tamil Nadu, INDIA

FIRST PUBLISHED ON THE OCCASION
of the
60TH JAYANTI
of
Bhagavan Sri Ramana Maharshi
27th December 1939

Bhagavan Sri Ramana Maharshi
(1879 - 1950)

Thou dost root out the ego of those who meditate on Thee in the Heart, Oh Arunachala!
— *Arunachala Aksharamanamalai*, v. 1

PREFACE

In response to the earnest desire of a large number of devotees of Bhagavan Sri Ramana, the answers to some of the questions put to Him from time to time are printed in a book-form under the title *MAHARSHI'S GOSPEL* for the benefit of the world at large.

These questions occur to ever so many of us, and we struggle within ourselves to solve them. The answers given by Maharshi are the quintessence of Divine Wisdom, based as they are on His direct knowledge and experience. His answers are of inestimable value to the earnest seeker of Truth.

The profound truth of Advaita that the one and only Reality is the Self absolute or Brahman, has nowhere been more lucidly expounded than in these pages. Because, on the one hand, it is on the basis of the highest experience that is His, that Bhagavan Sri Ramana speaks, and on the other, it is from the viewpoint of the common understanding of the layman that the aspirant seeks to know the Truth.

Truth is the same for one and all, and Sri Bhagavan directs the earnest aspirant to investigate and critically examine his own intimate experience and to seek for himself the core of his being, the Heart, which is eternally identical with the One Ultimate Reality, of which everything else seen or known is merely a phenomenal manifestation.

Every word that comes from the lips of the Sage is of the essence of *Upanishadic* wisdom, of which He is Himself the Supreme Embodiment.*

The devout reader will find in these pages practical advice, and will gain the conviction that his essential nature is Divine;

* The reader is referred to Sri Swami Siddheswarananda's Article on page 68.

CONTENTS

BOOK I

BOOK II

MAHARSHI'S GOSPEL

BOOK 1

1

Work and Renunciation

Disciple: What is the highest goal of spiritual experience for man?

Maharshi: Self-realization.

D: Can a married man realise the Self?

M: Certainly. Married or unmarried, a man can realise the Self; because That is here and now. If it were not so, but attainable by some effort at some time, and if it were new and had to be acquired, it would not be worth pursuit. Because, what is not natural is not permanent either. But what I say is that the Self is here and now, and alone.

D: A salt-doll diving into the sea will not be protected by a waterproof coat. This world in which we have to toil day in and day out is like the ocean.

M: Yes, the mind is the waterproof coat.

D: So then, one may be engaged in work and, free from desire, keep up one's solitude? But life's duties allow little time to sit in meditation or even to pray.

M: Yes. Work performed with attachment is a shackle, whereas work performed with detachment does not affect the doer. He is, even while working, in solitude. To engage in your duty is the true *namaskar*..... and abiding in God is the only true *asana*.

D: Should I not renounce my home?

M: If that had been your destiny the question would not have arisen.

D: Why then did you leave your home in your youth?

M: Nothing happens except by Divine dispensation. One's course of conduct in this life is determined by one's *prarabdha*.

D: Is it good to devote all my time to the search for the Self? If that is impossible, should I merely keep quiet?

M: If you can keep quiet, without engaging in any other pursuit, it is very good: If that cannot be done, where is the use of being quiet so far as realization is concerned? So long as a person is obliged to be active, let him not give up attempts to realise the Self.

D: Do not one's actions affect one in after-births?

M: Are you born now? Why do you think of other births? The fact is, there is neither birth nor death. Let him who is born think of death and the palliative thereof!

D: Can you show us the dead?

M: Did you know your kinsmen before their birth that you should seek to know them after their death?

D: How does a *grihastha* fare in the scheme of *moksha*? Should he not necessarily become a mendicant in order to attain liberation?

M: Why do you think you are a *grihastha*? Similar thoughts that you are a *sannyasin* will haunt you, even if you go out as a *sannyasin*. Whether you continue in the household or renounce it and go to the forest, your mind haunts you. The ego is the source of thought. It creates the body and the world, and it makes you think of being the *grihastha*. If you renounce, it will only substitute the thought of *sannyasa* for that of *grihastha*, and the environment of the forest for that of the household. But the mental obstacles are always there for you. They even increase greatly in the new surroundings. It is no help to change the environment. The one obstacle is the mind; it must be got over whether in the home or in the forest. If you can do it in the forest, why not in the home? Therefore, why change the environment? Your efforts can be made even now, whatever be the environment.

D: Is it possible to enjoy *samadhi* while busy in worldly work?

M: The feeling 'I work' is the hindrance. Ask yourself 'who works?' Remember who you are. Then the work will not bind you; it will go on automatically. Make no effort either to work or to renounce; your effort is the bondage. What is destined to happen will happen. If you are destined not to work, work cannot be had even if you hunt for it; if you are destined to work, you will not be able to avoid it; you will be forced to engage yourself in it. So, leave it to the higher power; you cannot renounce or retain as you choose.

D: Bhagavan said yesterday that while one is engaged in search of God 'within', 'outer' work would go on automatically. In the life of Sri Chaitanya it is said that during his lectures to students he was really seeking Krishna (Self) within, forgot all about his body and went on talking of Krishna only. This raises a doubt whether work can safely be left to itself. Should one keep part-attention on the physical work?

M: The Self is all. Are you apart from the Self? Or can the work go on without the Self? The Self is universal: so, all actions will go on whether you strain yourself to be engaged in them or not. The work will go on of itself. Thus Krishna told Arjuna that he need not trouble to kill the Kauravas; they were already slain by God. It was not for him to resolve to work and worry himself about it, but to allow his own nature to carry out the will of the higher power.

D: But the work may suffer if I do not attend to it.

M: Attending to the Self means attending to the work. Because you identify yourself with the body, you think that work is done by you. But the body and its activities, including that work, are not apart from the Self. What does it matter whether you attend to the work or not? Suppose you walk from one place to another: you do not attend to the steps you take. Yet you find yourself after a time at your goal. You see how the business of walking goes on without your attending to it. So also with other kinds of work.

D: It is then *like* sleep-walking.

M: *Like* somnambulism? Quite so. When a child is fast asleep, his mother feeds him; the child eats the food just as well as when he is fully awake. But the next morning he says to the mother, "Mother, I did not take food last night". The mother and others know that he did, but he says that he did not; he was not aware. Still the action had gone on.

A traveller in a cart has fallen asleep. The bulls move, stand still or are unyoked during the journey. He does not know these events but finds himself in a different place after he wakes up. He has been blissfully ignorant of the occurrences on the way, but the journey has been finished. Similarly with the Self of a person. The ever-wakeful Self is compared to the traveller asleep in the cart. The waking state is the moving of the bulls; *samadhi* is their standing still (because *samadhi* means *jagrat-sushupti*, that is to say, the person is aware but not concerned in the action; the bulls are yoked but do not move); sleep is the unyoking of the bulls, for there is complete stopping of activity corresponding to the relief of the bulls from the yoke.

Or again, take the instance of the cinema. Scenes are projected on the screen in the cinema-show. But the moving pictures do not affect or alter the screen. The spectator pays attention to them, not to the screen. They cannot exist apart from the screen, yet the screen is ignored. So also, the Self is the screen where the pictures, activities etc. are seen going on. The man is aware of the latter but not aware of the essential former. All the same the world of pictures is not apart from the Self. Whether he is aware of the screen or unaware, the actions will continue.

D: But there is an operator in the cinema!

M: The cinema-show is made out of insentient materials. The lamp, the pictures, the screen etc., are all insentient and so they need an operator, the sentient agent. On the other hand, the Self is absolute consciousness, and therefore self-contained. There cannot be an operator apart from the Self.

D: I am not confusing the body with the operator; rather, I am referring to Krishna's words in the 61st verse, Chapter XVIII of the *Gita*.

ईश्वरः सर्वभूतानां हृद्देशेऽर्जुन तिष्ठति ।
भ्रामयन्सर्वभूतानि यन्त्रारूढानि मायया ॥ [1]

M: The functions of the body involving the need for an operator, are borne in mind; since the body is *jada* or insentient, a sentient operator is necessary. Because people think that they are *jivas*, Krishna said that God resides in the heart as the operator of the *jivas*. In fact, there are no *jivas* and no operator, as it were, outside them; the Self comprises all. It is the screen, the pictures, the seer, the actors, the operator, the light, the theatre and all else. Your confounding the Self with the body and imagining yourself the actor, is like the seer representing himself as an actor in the cinema-show. *Imagine the actor asking if he can enact a scene without the screen*! Such is the case of the man who thinks of his actions apart from the Self.

D: On the other hand, *it is like asking the spectator to act in the cinema-picture*. So, we must learn sleep-waking!

M: Actions and states are according to one's point of view. A crow, an elephant, a snake, each makes use of one limb for two alternate purposes. With one eye the crow looks on either side; for the elephant the trunk serves the purpose of both a hand and a nose, and the serpent sees as well as hears with its eyes. Whether you say the crow has an eye or eyes, or refer to the trunk of the elephant as 'hand' or 'nose' or call the eyes of the serpent its ears, it means all the same. Similarly in the case of the *jnani*, sleep-waking or waking-sleep or dream-sleep or dreaming-wakefulness, are all much the same thing.

D: But we have to deal with a physical body in a physical, waking world! If we sleep while work is going on, or try to work while asleep, the work will go wrong.

M: Sleep is not ignorance, it is one's pure state; wakefulness is not knowledge, it is ignorance. There is full awareness in sleep and total ignorance in waking. Your real nature covers both and

---

[1] "The Lord, O Arjuna, dwells in the Heart of every being, and He by His delusive power spins round all beings set as if on a machine".

extends beyond. The Self is beyond both knowledge and ignorance. Sleep, dream and waking states are only modes passing before the Self: they proceed whether you are aware of them or not. That is the state of the *jnani*, in whom pass the states of *samadhi*, waking, dream and deep sleep, like the bulls moving, standing, or being unyoked, while the passenger is asleep. These answers are from the point of view of the *ajnani*; otherwise such questions would not arise.

D: Of course, they cannot arise for the Self. Who would be there to ask? But unfortunately, I have not yet realised the Self!

M: That is just the obstacle in your way. You must get rid of the idea that you are an *ajnani* and have yet to realise the Self. You are the Self. Was there ever a time when you were not aware of that Self?

D: So, we must experiment in sleep-waking ..... or in day-dreaming?

M: (Laughs).

D: I maintain that the physical body of the man immersed in *samadhi* as a result of the unbroken 'contemplation'[2] of the Self, may become motionless for that reason. It may be active or inactive. The mind established in such 'contemplation' will not be affected by the movements of the body or the senses; nor is disturbance of the mind the forerunner of physical activity. Whereas another person asserts that physical activity certainly prevents *samadhi* or unbroken 'contemplation'. What is Bhagavan's opinion? You are the abiding proof of my statement.

M: Both of you are right: you refer to *sahaja nirvikalpa samadhi* and the other refers to *kevala nirvikalpa samadhi*. In the latter case the mind lies immersed in the light of the Self (whereas, the mind lies in the darkness of ignorance in deep sleep); and the subject makes a distinction between *samadhi* and activity after waking up from *samadhi*. Moreover, activity of the body,

---

[2] The word, contemplation, is often used loosely as referring to a forced mental process, whereas *samadhi* lies beyond effort. However, in the language of Christian mysticism "contemplation" is the synonym invariably used for *samadhi*, and it is in this sense the word is used above.

of the sight, of the vital forces and of the mind and the cognisance of objects, all these are obstructions for one who seeks to realise *kevala nirvikalpa samadhi.*

In *sahaja samadhi*, however, the mind has resolved into the Self and has been lost. The differences and obstructions mentioned above do not, therefore, exist here. The activities of such a being are like the feeding of a somnolent boy, perceptible to the onlooker but not to the subject. The traveller sleeping in the moving cart is not aware of the motion of the cart, because his mind is sunk in darkness. Whereas, the *sahaja jnani* remains unaware of his bodily activities because his mind is dead, having been resolved into the ecstasy of *chidananda* (bliss of the Self).

Note: The distinction between sleep, *kevala nirvikalpa samadhi and sahaja nirvikalpa samadhi* can be clearly put in a tabular form as given by Sri Bhagavan:

Sleep	*Kevala Nirvikalpa Samadhi*	*Sahaja Nirvikalpa Samadhi*
1) mind alive	1) mind alive	1) mind dead
2) sunk in oblivion	2) sunk in Light	2) resolved into the Self
	3) like a bucket tied to a rope and left lying in the water in a well	3) like a river discharged into the ocean and its identity lost
	4) to be drawn out by the other end of the rope	4) a river cannot be redirected from the ocean

The mind of the Sage who has realized the Self is wholly destroyed. It is dead. But to the onlooker, he may seem to possess a mind just like the layman. Hence the 'I' in the Sage has merely an apparent 'objective reality'. In fact however, it has neither a subjective existence nor an objective reality.

11

Silence and Solitude

D: Is a vow of silence useful?

M: The inner silence is self-surrender. And that is living without the sense of ego.

D: Is solitude necessary for a *sannyasin*?

M: Solitude is in the mind of a man. One might be in the thick of the world and yet maintain perfect serenity of mind; such a person is always in solitude. Another may stay in the forest, but still be unable to control his mind. He cannot be said to be in solitude. Solitude is an attitude of the mind; a man attached to the things of life cannot get solitude, wherever he may be. A detached man is always in solitude.

D: What is *mauna*?

M: That state which transcends speech and thought is *mauna*; it is meditation without mental activity. Subjugation of the mind is meditation; deep meditation is eternal speech. Silence is ever-speaking; it is the perennial flow of 'language'. It is interrupted by speaking; for words obstruct this mute 'language'. Lectures may entertain individuals for hours without improving them. Silence, on the other hand, is permanent and benefits the whole of humanity. . . . . . By silence, eloquence is meant. Oral lectures are not so eloquent as silence. Silence is unceasing eloquence. . . . It is the best language.

There is a state when words cease and silence prevails.

D: How then can we communicate our thoughts to one another?

M: That becomes necessary if the sense of duality exists....

D: Why does not Bhagavan go about and preach the Truth to the people at large?

M: How do you know I am not doing it? Does preaching consist in mounting a platform and haranguing the people around? Preaching is simple communication of knowledge; it can really be done in silence only. What do you think of a man who listens to a sermon for an hour and goes away without having been impressed by it so as to change his life? Compare him with another, who sits in a holy presence and goes away after sometime with his outlook on life totally changed. Which is the better, to preach loudly without effect or to sit silently sending out inner force?

Again, how does speech arise? There is abstract knowledge, whence arises the ego, which in turn gives rise to thought, and thought to the spoken word. So the word is the great-grandson of the original source. If the word can produce effect, judge for yourself, how much more powerful must be the preaching through silence! But people do not understand this simple, bare truth, the truth of their everyday, ever-present, eternal experience. This truth is that of the Self. Is there anyone unaware of the Self? But they do not like even to hear of this truth, whereas they are eager to know what lies beyond, about heaven, hell and reincarnation.

Because they love mystery and not the truth, religions cater to them so as eventually to bring them round to the Self. Whatever be the means adopted, you must at last return to the Self: so why not abide in the Self here and now? To be a spectator of, or to speculate about the other world, the Self is necessary; therefore, they are not different from the Self. Even the ignorant man when he sees the objects, sees only the Self.

III

Mind Control

D: How can I control the mind?

M: There is no mind to control if the Self is realised. The Self shines forth when the mind vanishes. In the realised man the mind may be active or inactive, the Self alone exists. For, the mind, body and world are not separate from the Self; and they cannot remain apart from the Self. Can they be other than the Self? When aware of the Self why should one worry about these shadows? How do they affect the Self?

D: If the mind is merely a shadow how then is one to know the Self?

M: The Self is the heart, self-luminous. Illumination arises from the heart and reaches the brain, which is the seat of the mind. The world is seen with the mind; so you see the world by the reflected light of the Self. The world is perceived by an act of the mind. When the mind is illumined it is aware of the world; when it is not so illumined, it is not aware of the world.

If the mind is turned in, towards the source of illumination, objective knowledge ceases, and the Self alone shines as the heart.

The moon shines by reflecting the light of the sun. When the sun has set, the moon is useful for displaying objects. When the sun has risen no one needs the moon, though its disc is visible in the sky. So it is with the mind and the heart. The mind is made useful by its reflected light. It is used for seeing objects. When turned inwards, it merges into the source of illumination which shines by Itself and the mind is then like the moon in the daytime.

When it is dark, a lamp is necessary to give light. But when the sun has arisen, there is no need for the lamp; the objects are visible. And to see the sun no lamp is necessary; it is enough if you turn your eyes towards the self-luminous sun. Similarly with the mind; to see the objects the light reflected from the mind is necessary. To see the heart it is enough that the mind is turned towards it. Then the mind does not count and the heart is self-effulgent.

D: After leaving this Ashram in October, I was aware of the Presence that prevails in Sri Bhagavan's presence enfolding me for about ten days. All the time, while busy in my work, there was an undercurrent of that peace in unity; it was almost like the dual consciousness which one experiences while half-asleep in a dull lecture. Then, it faded out entirely, and the old stupidities came in instead. Work leaves no time for separate meditation. Is it enough constantly reminding oneself 'I AM', while at work?

M: *(After a short pause).* If you strengthen the mind, that peace will continue for all time. Its duration is proportional to the strength of mind acquired by repeated practice. And such a mind is able to hold on to the current. In that case, engagement or no engagement in work, the current remains unaffected and uninterrupted. It is not the work that hinders but the idea that it is you who are doing it.

D: Is a set meditation necessary for strengthening the mind?

M: Not if you keep the idea always before you that it is not your work. At first, effort is needed to remind yourself of it, but later on it becomes natural and continuous. The work will go on of its own accord, and your peace will remain undisturbed.

Meditation is your true nature. You call it meditation now, because there are other thoughts distracting you. When these thoughts are dispelled, you remain alone — that is, in the state of meditation free from thoughts; and that is your real nature, which you are now trying to gain by keeping away other thoughts. Such keeping away of other thoughts is now called meditation. But when the practice becomes firm, the real nature shows itself as true meditation.

D: Other thoughts arise more forcibly when one attempts meditation!

M: Yes, all kinds of thought arise in meditation. That is only right; for what lies hidden in you is brought out. Unless it rises up, how can it be destroyed? Thoughts rise up spontaneously, as it were, but only to be extinguished in due course, thus strengthening the mind.

D: There are times when persons and things take a vague, almost a transparent form, as in a dream. One ceases to observe them as outside, but is passively conscious of their existence, while not actively conscious of any kind of selfhood. There is a deep quietness in the mind. Is it at such times that one is ready to dive into the Self? Or is this condition unhealthy, the result of self-hypnotism? Should it be encouraged as yielding temporary peace?

M: There is Consciousness along with quietness in the mind; this is exactly the state to be aimed at. The fact that the question has been framed on this point, without realizing that it is the Self, shows that the state is not steady but casual.

The word 'diving' is appropriate when there are outgoing tendencies, and when, therefore, the mind has to be directed and turned within, there is a dip below the surface of externalities. But when quietness prevails without obstructing the Consciousness, where is the need to dive? If that state has not been realised as the Self, the effort to do so may be called 'diving'. In this sense the state may be said to be suitable for realization or diving. Thus, the last two questions you have put do not arise.

D: The mind continues to feel partial towards children possibly because the form of a child is often used to personify the Ideal. How can this preference be outgrown?

M: Hold on to the Self. Why think of children and of your reactions towards them?

D: This third visit to Tiruvannamalai seems to have intensified the sense of egoism in me and made meditation less easy. Is this an unimportant passing phase or a sign that I should avoid such places hereafter?

M: It is imaginary. This place or another is within you. Such imaginations must end; for places as such have nothing to do with the activities of the mind. Also your surroundings are not merely a matter of your individual choice; they are there, as a matter of course; and you should rise above them and not get yourself entangled in them.

(A boy of eight and a half years sat in the hall at about five in the evening, when Sri Bhagavan went up the Hill. During His absence, the boy spoke on *yoga* and *Vedanta* in pure, simple and literary Tamil, quoting freely from the sayings of saints and the sacred scriptures. When Sri Bhagavan entered the hall, after nearly three-quarters of an hour, only silence prevailed. For the twenty minutes the boy sat in Sri Bhagavan's presence, he spoke not a word but was merely gazing at Him. Then tears flowed from his eyes. He wiped them with his left hand and soon after left the place saying that he still awaits Self-realization).

D: How should we explain the extraordinary characteristics of the boy?

M: The characteristics of his last birth are strong in him. But however strong they may be, they do not manifest themselves save in a calm, still mind. It is within the experience of all, that attempts to revive memory sometimes fail, while something flashes into the mind when it is calm and quiet.

D: How can the rebellious mind be made calm and tranquil?

M: Either see its source so that it may disappear, or surrender yourself so that it may be struck down. Self-surrender is the same as Self-knowledge, and either of them necessarily implies self-control. The ego submits only when it recognises the Higher Power.

D: How can I escape from *samsara* which seems to be the real cause for making the mind restless? Is not renunciation an effective means to realise tranquillity of mind?

M: *Samsara* is only in your mind. The world does not speak out saying, 'Here I am, the world'. If it did so, it would be ever there, making its presence felt by you even in your sleep. Since, however, it is not there in sleep, it is impermanent. Being impermanent, it lacks substance. Having no reality apart from the Self it is easily subdued by the Self. The Self alone is permanent. Renunciation is the non-identification of the Self with the not-Self. When the ignorance which identifies the Self with not-Self is removed, not-Self ceases to exist, and that is true renunciation.

D: Can we not perform actions without attachment even in the absence of such renunciation?

M: An *atma jnani* alone can be a good *karma yogi.*

D: Does Bhagavan condemn *dvaita* Philosophy?

M: *Dvaita* can subsist only when you identify the Self with the not-Self. *Advaita* is non-identification.

IV

Bhakti and Jnana

D: *Sri Bhagavata* outlines a way to find Krishna in the heart by prostrating to all and looking on all as the Lord Himself. Is this the right path leading to Self-realization? Is it not easier thus to adore Bhagavan in whatever meets the 'mind', than to seek the supramental through the mental enquiry, Who am I?

M: Yes, when you see God in all, do you think of God or do you not? You must certainly think of God for seeing God all round you. Keeping God in your mind becomes *dhyana* and *dhyana* is the stage before Realization. Realization can only be in and of the Self. It can never be apart from the Self: and *dhyana* must precede it. Whether you make *dhyana* on God or on the Self, it is immaterial; for the goal is the same. You cannot, by any means, escape the Self. You want to see God in all, but not in yourself? If *all* is God, are you not included in that *all*? Being God yourself, is it a wonder that all is God? This is the method advised in *Sri Bhagavata*, and elsewhere by others. But even for this practice there must be the seer or thinker. Who is he?

D: How to see God who is all-pervasive?

M: To see God is to *be* God. There is no 'all' apart from God for Him to pervade. He alone *is*.

D: Should we read *Gita* now and then?

M: Always.

D: What is the relation between *jnana* and *bhakti*?

M: The eternal, unbroken, natural state of abiding in the Self is *jnana*. To abide in the Self you must love the Self. Since God is verily the Self, love of the Self is love of God; and that is *bhakti*. *Jnana* and *bhakti* are thus one and the same.

D: While doing *nama japa* for an hour or more I fall into a state like sleep. On waking up I recollect that my *japa* has been interrupted. So, I try again.

M: 'Like sleep', that is right. It is the natural state. Because you are now associated with the ego, you consider that the natural state is something which interrupts your work. So you must have the experience repeated until you realise that it is your natural state. You will then find that *japa* is extraneous but still it will go on automatically. Your present doubt is due to that false identity, namely of identifying yourself with the mind that does the *japa*. *Japa* means clinging to one thought to the exclusion of all other thoughts. That is its purpose. It leads to *dhyana* which ends in Self-realization or *jnana*.

D: How should I carry on *nama japa*?

M: One should not use the name of God mechanically and superficially without the feeling of devotion. To use the name of God one must call upon Him with yearning and unreservedly surrender oneself to Him. Only after such surrender is the name of God constantly with the man.

D: Where is, then, the need for enquiry or *vichara*?

M: Surrender can take effect only when it is done with full knowledge as to what real surrender means. Such knowledge comes after enquiry and reflection and ends invariably in self-surrender. There is no difference between *jnana* and absolute surrender to the Lord, that is, in thought, word and deed. To be complete, surrender must be unquestioning; the devotee cannot bargain with the Lord or demand favours at His hands. Such entire surrender comprises all; it is *jnana* and *vairagya*, devotion and love.

V

Self and Individuality

D: Does not death dissolve the individuality of a person, so that there can be no rebirth, just as the rivers discharged into the ocean lose their individualities?

M: But when the waters evaporate and return as rain on the hills, they once more flow in the form of rivers and fall into the ocean; so also the individualities during sleep lose their separateness and yet return as individuals according to their *samskaras* or past tendencies. Even so it is in death; and the individuality of the person with *samskaras* is not lost.

D: How can that be?

M: See how a tree whose branches have been cut, grows again. So long as the roots of the tree remain unimpaired, the tree will continue to grow. Similarly, the *samskaras* which have merely sunk into the heart on death, but have not perished for that reason, occasion rebirth at the right time; and that is how *jivas* are reborn.

D: How could the innumerable *jivas* and the wide universe whose existence is correlative to that of the *jivas*, sprout up from such subtle *samskaras* sunk in the heart?

M: Just as the big banyan tree sprouts from a tiny seed, so do the *jivas* and the whole universe with name and form sprout up from the subtle *samskaras*.

D: How does individuality emanate from the Absolute Self, and how is its return made possible?

M: As a spark proceeds from fire, individuality emanates from the Absolute Self. The spark is called the ego. In the case of the *ajnani*, the ego identifies itself with some object simultaneously with its rise. It cannot remain without such association with objects.

This association is due to *ajnana*, whose destruction is the objective of one's efforts. If this tendency to identify itself with objects is destroyed, the ego becomes pure and then it also merges into its source. The false identification of oneself with the body is *dehatma-buddhi* or 'I-am-the-body'-idea. This must go before good results can follow.

D: How am I to eradicate it?

M: You exist in *sushupti* without being associated with the body and the mind, but in the other two states you are associated with them. If you were one with the body, how could you exist without the body in *sushupti*? You can separate yourself from what is external to you but not from that which is one with you. Hence the ego cannot be one with the body. This must be realised in the waking state. The three states are studied in order to gain this knowledge.

D: How can the ego which is confined to two of the states endeavour to realise That which comprises all the three states?

M: The ego in its purity is experienced in the intervals between two states or between two thoughts. The ego is like the worm which leaves one hold only after it catches another. Its true nature is known when it is out of contact with objects or thoughts. You should realise this interval as the abiding, unchangeable Reality, your true Being, through the conviction gained by the study of the three states, *jagrat, svapna and sushupti.*

D: Can I not remain in *sushupti* as long as I like and also be in it at will, just as I am in the waking state? What is the *jnani's* experience of these three states?

M: *Sushupti* does exist in your waking state also. You are in *sushupti* even now. That should be consciously entered into and reached in this very waking state. There is no real going in and coming out of it. To be aware of *sushupti* in the *jagrat* state is *jagrat-sushupti* and that is *samadhi.*

The *ajnani* cannot remain long in *sushupti*, because he is forced by his nature to emerge from it. His ego is not dead and it will rise again and again. But the *jnani* crushes the ego at its source. It may seem to emerge at times in his case also as if impelled by *prarabdha*. That is, in the case of the *jnani* also, for all outward purposes *prarabdha* would seem to sustain or keep up the ego, as in the case of the *ajnani*; but there is this fundamental difference, that the *ajnani's* ego when it rises up (really it has not subsided except in deep sleep) is quite ignorant of its source; in other words, the *ajnani* is not aware of his *sushupti* in his dream and waking states; in the case of the *jnani*, on the contrary, the rise or existence of the ego is only apparent, and he enjoys his unbroken, transcendental experience in spite of such apparent rise or existence of the ego, keeping his attention (*lakshya*) always on the Source. This ego is harmless; it is merely like the skeleton of a burnt rope — though with a form, it is useless to tie up anything. By constantly keeping one's attention on the Source, the ego is dissolved in that Source like a salt-doll in the sea.

D: What is the significance of the Crucifixion?

M: The body is the cross. Jesus, the son of man, is the ego or 'I-am-the-body'-idea. When the son of man is crucified on the cross, the ego perishes, and what survives is the Absolute Being. It is the resurrection of the glorious Self, of the Christ — the son of God.

D: But how is crucifixion justified? Is not killing a terrible crime?

M: Everyone is committing suicide. The eternal, blissful, natural state has been smothered by this ignorant life. In this way the present life is due to the killing of the eternal, positive existence. Is it not really a case of suicide? So, why worry about killing etc.?

D: Sri Ramakrishna says that *nirvikalpa samadhi* cannot last longer than twenty-one days; if persisted in, the person dies. Is this a fact?

M: When the *prarabdha* is exhausted, the ego is completely dissolved, without leaving any trace behind. This is the final liberation (*nirvana*). Unless *prarabdha* is exhausted, the ego will rise up as it *may appear* to do in the case of *jivanmuktas*.

VI

Self-Realisation

D: How can I attain Self-realization?

M: Realization is nothing to be gained afresh, it is already there. All that is necessary is to get rid of the thought 'I have not realised'.

Stillness or peace is Realization. There is no moment when the Self is not. So long as there is doubt or the feeling of non-realization, the attempt should be made to rid oneself of these thoughts. They are due to the identification of the Self with the not-Self. When the not-Self disappears, the Self alone remains. To make room, it is enough that the cramping be removed; room is not brought in from elsewhere.

D: Since Realization is not possible without *vasana-kshaya*, how am I to realise that State in which the *vasanas* are effectively destroyed?

M: You are in that State now!

D: Does it mean that by holding on to the Self, the *vasanas* should be destroyed as and when they emerge?

M: They will themselves be destroyed if you remain as you are.

D: How shall I reach the Self?

M: There is no reaching the Self. If Self were to be reached, it would mean that the Self is not here and now but that it is yet to be obtained. What is got afresh will also be lost. So it will be impermanent. What is not permanent is not worth striving for. So I say the Self is not reached. You *are* the Self; you are already That.

The fact is, you are ignorant of your blissful state. Ignorance supervenes and draws a veil over the pure Self which is Bliss.

Attempts are directed only to remove this veil of ignorance which is merely wrong knowledge. The wrong knowledge is the false identification of the Self with the body, mind etc. This False identification must go, and then the Self alone remains.

Therefore Realization is for everyone; Realization makes no difference between the aspirants. This very doubt, whether you can realise, and the notion 'I-have-not-realised' are themselves the obstacles. Be free from these obstacles also.

D: What is the use of *samadhi* and does thought subsist then?

M: *Samadhi* alone can reveal the Truth. Thoughts cast a veil over Reality, and so It is not realised as such in states other than *samadhi*.

In *samadhi* there is only the feeling 'I AM' and no thoughts. The experience 'I AM' is being still.

D: How can I repeat the experience of *samadhi* or the stillness that I obtain here?

M: Your present experience is due to the influence of the atmosphere in which you find yourself. Can you have it outside this atmosphere? The experience is spasmodic. Until it becomes permanent, practice is necessary.

D: One has at times vivid flashes of a consciousness whose centre is *outside* the *normal self*, and which seems to be all-inclusive. Without concerning ourselves with philosophical concepts, how would Bhagavan advise me to work towards *getting*, *retaining* and *extending* those rare flashes? Does *abhyasa* in such experience involve *retirement*?

M: *Outside*! For whom is the inside or outside? These can exist only so long as there are the subject and object. For whom are these two again? On investigation you will find that they resolve into the subject only. See who is the subject; and this enquiry leads you to pure Consciousness beyond the subject.

The *normal self* is the mind. This mind is with limitations. But pure Consciousness is beyond limitations, and is reached by investigation as above outlined.

Getting: The Self is always there. You have only to remove the veil obstructing the revelation of the Self.

Retaining: Once you realise the Self, it becomes your direct and immediate experience. It is never lost.

Extending: There is no extending of the Self, for it is as ever, without contraction or expansion.

Retirement: Abiding in the Self is solitude. Because there is nothing alien to the Self. Retirement must be from some one place or state to another. There is neither the one nor the other apart from the Self. *All* being the Self, retirement is impossible and inconceivable.

Abhyasa is only the prevention of disturbance to the inherent peace. You are always in your natural State whether you do *abhyasa* or not.... To remain as you are, without question or doubt, is your natural State.

D: On realizing *samadhi*, does not one obtain *siddhis* also?

M: In order to display *siddhis*, there must be others to recognise them. That means, there is no *jnana* in the one who displays them. Therefore, *siddhis* are not worth a thought; *jnana* alone is to be aimed at and gained.

D: Does my Realization help others?

M: Yes, and it is the best help that you can possibly render to others. Those who have discovered great truths have done so in the still depths of the Self. But really there are no 'others' to be helped. For, the Realised Being sees only the Self, just as the goldsmith sees only the gold while valuing it in various jewels made of gold. When you identify yourself with the body, name and form are there. But when you transcend the body-consciousness, the 'others' also disappear. The Realised one does not see the world as different from Himself.

D: Would it not be better if the saints mix with others?

M: There are no 'others' to mix with. The Self is the only Reality.

D: Should I not try to help the suffering world?

M: The Power that created you has created the world as well. If it can take care of you, it can similarly take care of the world also .... if God has created the world, it is His business to look after it, not yours.

D: Is it not our duty to be patriots?

M: Your duty is *to be* and not, to be this or that. 'I AM THAT I AM' sums up the whole truth; the method is summarised in '*be still*'.

And what does stillness mean? It means 'destroy yourself'; because, every name and form is the cause of trouble. 'I-I' is the Self. 'I am this' is the ego. When the 'I' is kept up as the 'I' only, it is the Self. When it flies off at a tangent and says 'I am this or that, I am such and such', it is the ego.

D: Who then is God?

M: The Self is God. 'I AM' is God. If God be apart from the Self, He must be a Selfless God, which is absurd. All that is required to realise the Self is to *be still.* What can be easier than that? Hence *atma vidya* is the easiest to attain.

VII

Guru and His Grace

D: What is *guru kripa*? How does it lead to Self-realization?

M: Guru is the Self.... Sometimes in his life a man becomes dissatisfied with it, and, not content with what he has, he seeks the satisfaction of his desires, through prayer to God etc. His mind is gradually purified until he longs to know God, more to obtain His grace than to satisfy his worldly desires. Then, God's grace begins to manifest. God takes the form of a Guru and appears to the devotee, teaches him the Truth and, moreover, purifies his mind by association. The devotee's mind gains strength and is then able to turn inward. By meditation it is further purified and it remains still without the least ripple. That calm expanse is the Self.

The Guru is both 'external' and 'internal'. From the 'exterior' he gives a push to the mind to turn inward; from the 'interior' He pulls the mind towards the Self and helps in the quieting of the mind. That is *guru kripa*. There is no difference between God, Guru and the Self.

D: In the Theosophical Society they meditate in order to seek Masters to guide them.

M: The Master is within. Meditation is meant to remove the ignorant idea that He is only outside. If He be a stranger whom you await, He is bound to disappear also. Where is the use for a transient being like that? But as long as you think you are separate or that you are the body, so long is the Master 'without' also necessary, and He will appear as if with a body. When the wrong identification of oneself with the body ceases, the Master will be found as none other than the Self.

D: Will the Guru help us to know the Self through initiation etc.?

M: Does the Guru hold you by the hand and whisper in the ear? You may imagine him to be what you are yourself. Because you think you are with a body, you think He also has a body to do something tangible for you. His work lies within, in the spiritual realm.

D: How is the Guru found?

M: God, who is immanent, in His grace takes pity on the loving devotee and manifests Himself according to the devotee's development. The devotee thinks that He is a man and expects a relationship as between two physical bodies. But the Guru, who is God or the Self incarnate, works from within, helps the man to see the error of his ways and guides him in the right path until he realises the Self within.

D: What should the devotee do then?

M: He has only to act up to the words of the Master and work within. The Master is both 'within' and 'without', so He creates conditions to drive you inward and at the same time prepares the 'interior' to drag you to the Centre. Thus He gives a push from 'without' and exerts a pull from 'within', so that you may be fixed at the Centre.

You think that the world can be conquered by your own efforts. When you are frustrated externally and are driven inwards, you feel 'Oh! there is a Power higher than man!'

The ego is like a very powerful elephant which cannot be brought under control by any less powerful than a lion, which, in this instance, is no other than the Guru, whose very look makes the elephant-like ego tremble and die.

You will know in due course that your glory lies where you cease to exist. In order to gain that state, you should surrender yourself. Then the Master sees that you are in a fit state to receive guidance, and He guides you.

D: How can the silence of the Guru, who gives no initiation nor does any other tangible act, be more powerful than His word etc.? How is such silence better than the study of scriptures?

M: Silence is the most potent form of work. However vast and emphatic the scriptures may be, they fail in their effect. The Guru is quiet and Grace prevails in all. This silence is more vast and more emphatic than all the scriptures put together.

D: But can the devotee obtain happiness?

M: The devotee surrenders himself to the Master and it means that there is no vestige of individuality retained by him. If the surrender is complete, all sense of self is lost, and then there can be no misery or sorrow.

The eternal Being is nothing but happiness. That comes as a revelation.

D: How can I obtain Grace?

M: Grace is the Self. That also is not to be acquired; you only need to know that it exists.

The sun is brightness only. It does not see darkness. Yet you speak of darkness fleeing on the sun's approach. So also the devotee's ignorance, like the phantom of darkness, vanishes at the look of the Guru. You are surrounded by sunlight; yet if you want to see the sun, you must turn in its direction and look at it. So also Grace is found by the proper approach you make, though it is here and now.

D: Cannot Grace hasten ripeness in the seeker?

M: Leave it all to the Master. Surrender to Him without reserve.

One of two things must be done: either surrender yourself, because you realise your inability and need a higher power to help you; or investigate into the cause of misery, go into the Source and so merge in the Self. Either way, you will be free from misery. God or Guru never forsakes the devotee who has surrendered himself.

D: What is the significance of prostration to the Guru or God?

M: Prostration signifies the subsidence of the ego, and it means merging into the Source. God or Guru cannot be deceived by outward genuflexions, bowing and prostrations. He sees whether the ego is there or not.

D: Will not Bhagavan give me some *prasad* from His leaf as a mark of His Grace?

M: Eat without thinking of the ego. Then what you eat becomes Bhagavan's *prasad.*

D: Is not the literate man better qualified for Enlightenment in the sense that he stands in no need of *guru kripa*?

M: Even a learned man must bow before the illiterate sage. Illiteracy is ignorance and education is learned ignorance. Both are ignorant of the true aim. The Sage is ignorant in a different line. He is ignorant because there is no 'other' for Him.

D: Is it not to obtain the Guru's Grace that presents are offered to Him? So, the visitors offer presents to Bhagavan.

M: Why do they bring presents? Do I want them? Even if I refuse, they thrust the presents on me! What for? Is it not like giving a bait to catch the fish? Is the angler anxious to feed them? No, he is anxious to feed on the fish!

D: Is the Theosophical idea of giving successive initiations before attaining *moksha* true ?

M: Those who attain *moksha* in one life must have passed through all the initiations in their former lives.

D: Theosophy says that *jnanis* after death have to choose four or five lines of work, not necessarily in this world. What is Bhagavan's opinion?

M: Some may take up work, but not all.

D: Are you conscious of a brotherhood of invisible *Rishis*?

M: If invisible, how can you see them?

D: In consciousness.

M: There is nothing external in Consciousness.

D: Can I realise them?

M: If you realise your own Reality, then that of the *Rishis* and Masters will become clear to you. There is only one Master, and that is the Self.

D: Is reincarnation true?

M: Reincarnation exists only so long as there is ignorance.

There is really no reincarnation at all, either now or before. Nor will there be any hereafter. This is the truth.

D: Can a *yogi* know his past lives?

M: Do you know the present life that you wish to know the past? Find the present, then the rest will follow. Even with our present limited knowledge, you suffer so much; why should you burden yourself with more knowledge? Is it to suffer more?

D: Does Bhagavan use occult powers to make others realise the Self, or is the mere fact of Bhagavan's Realization enough for that?

M: The spiritual force of Self-realization is far more powerful than the use of all the occult powers. Inasmuch as there is no ego in the Sage, there are no 'others' for Him. What is the highest benefit that can be conferred on you? It is happiness, and happiness is born of peace. Peace can reign only where there is no disturbance, and disturbance is due to thoughts that arise in the mind. When the mind itself is absent, there will be perfect peace. Unless a person has annihilated the mind, he cannot gain peace and be happy. And unless he himself be happy, he cannot bestow happiness on 'others'. Since however there are no 'others' for the Sage who has no mind, the mere fact of His Self-realization is itself enough to make the 'others' happy.

VIII

Peace and Happiness

D: How can I get peace? I do not seem to obtain it through *vichara*.

M: Peace is your natural state. It is the mind that obstructs the natural state. Your *vichara* has been made only in the mind. Investigate what the mind is, and it will disappear. There is no such thing as mind apart from thought. Nevertheless, because of the emergence of thought, you surmise something from which it starts and term that the mind. When you probe to see what it is, you find there is really no such thing as mind. When the mind has thus vanished, you realise eternal peace.

D: Through poetry, music, *japa*, *bhajana*, the sight of beautiful landscapes, reading the lines of spiritual verses etc., one experiences sometimes a true sense of all-unity. Is that feeling of deep blissful quiet (wherein the personal self has no place) the same as the entering into the heart of which Bhagavan speaks? Will practice thereof lead to a deeper *samadhi* and so ultimately to a full vision of the Real?

M: There is happiness when agreeable things are presented to the mind. It is the happiness inherent to the Self, and there is no other happiness. And it is not alien and afar. You are diving into the Self on those occasions which you consider pleasurable; that diving results in self-existent bliss. But the association of ideas is responsible for foisting that bliss on other things or occurrences while, in fact, that bliss is within you. On these occasions you are plunging into the Self, though unconsciously. If you do so consciously, with the conviction that comes of the experience that you are identical with the happiness which is verily the Self, the one Reality, you call it Realization. I want you to dive consciously into the Self, *i.e.*, into the heart.

MAHARSHI'S GOSPEL

BOOK II

1

Self-Enquiry

Disciple: How is one to realise the Self?

Maharshi: Whose Self? Find out.

D: Mine, but who am I?

M: Find out yourself.

D: I don't know how.

M: Just think over the question. Who is it that says "I don't know"? Who is the 'I' in your statement? What is not known?

D: Somebody or something in me.

M: Who is that somebody? In whom?

D: Perhaps some power.

M: Find out.

D: Why was I born?

M: Who was born? The answer is the same to all your questions.

D: Who am I, then?

M: (Smiling.) You have come to examine me? You must say who you are.

D: However much I may try, I do not seem to catch the 'I'. It is not even clearly discernible.

M: Who is it that says that the 'I' is not discernible? Are there two 'I's in you that one is not discernible by the other?

D: Instead of enquiring 'Who am I?', can I put the question to myself 'Who are *You*?', since then, my mind may be fixed on You whom I consider to be God in the form of Guru. Perhaps, I would be nearer the goal of my quest by that enquiry than by asking myself 'Who am I?'

M: Whatever form your enquiry may take, you must finally come to the one I, the Self.

All these distinctions made between the 'I' and 'you', Master and disciple etc. are merely a sign of one's ignorance. The 'I-Supreme' alone is. To think otherwise is to delude oneself.

A *Puranic* story of Sage Ribhu and his disciple Nidagha, is particularly instructive in this context.

Although Ribhu taught his disciple the supreme Truth of the One Brahman without a second, Nidagha, in spite of his erudition and understanding, did not get sufficient conviction to adopt and follow the path of *jnana*, but settled down in his native town to lead a life devoted to the observance of ceremonial religion.

But the Sage loved his disciple as deeply as the latter venerated his Master. In spite of his age, Ribhu would himself go to his disciple in the town, just to see how far the latter had outgrown his ritualism. At times the Sage went in disguise, so that he might observe how Nidagha would act when he did not know that he was being observed by his Master.

On one such occasion Ribhu, who had put on the disguise of a village rustic, found Nidagha intently watching a royal procession. Unrecognised by the town dweller Nidagha, the village rustic enquired what the bustle was all about, and was told that the king was going in procession.

"Oh! It is the king. He goes in procession! But where is he?" asked the rustic.

"There, on the elephant", said Nidagha.

"You say the king is on the elephant. Yes, I see the two", said the rustic, "But which is the king and which is the elephant?"

"What!" exclaimed Nidagha, "You see the two, but do not know that the man above is the king and the animal below is the elephant? Where is the use of talking to a man like you?"

"Pray, be not impatient with an ignorant man like me", begged the rustic. "But you said 'above' and 'below', what do they mean?"

Nidagha could stand it no more. "You see the king and the elephant, the one *above* and the other *below*. Yet you want to know what is meant by 'above' and 'below'?" burst out Nidagha. "If things seen and words spoken can convey so little to you, action alone can teach you. Bend forward, and you will know it all too well".

The rustic did as he was told. Nidagha got on his shoulders and said "Know it now. I am *above* as the king, you are *below* as the elephant. Is that clear enough?"

"No, not yet", was the rustic's quiet reply. "You say you are above like the king, and I am below like the elephant. The 'king', the 'elephant', 'above' and 'below', so far it is clear. But pray, tell me what you mean by 'I' and 'you'?"

When Nidagha was thus confronted all of a sudden with the mighty problem of defining the 'you' apart from the 'I', light dawned on his mind. At once he jumped down and fell at his Master's feet saying, "Who else but my venerable Master, Ribhu, could have thus drawn my mind from the superficialities of physical existence to the true Being of the Self? Oh, benign Master, I crave thy blessings".

Therefore, while your aim is to transcend here and now these superficialities of physical existence through *atma vichara*, where is the scope for making the distinctions of 'you' and 'I', which pertain only to the body? When you turn the mind within, seeking the source of thought, where is the 'you' and where is the 'I'?

You should seek and be the Self that includes all.

D: But is it not funny that the 'I' should be searching for the 'I'? Does not the enquiry, 'Who am I?' turn out in the end an empty formula? Or, am I to put the question to myself endlessly, repeating it like some *mantra*?

M: Self-enquiry is certainly not an empty formula; it is more than the repetition of any *mantra*. If the enquiry, 'Who am I?' were a mere mental questioning, it would not be of much value. The very purpose of Self-enquiry is to focus the entire mind at its source. It is not, therefore, a case of one 'I' searching for another 'I'.

Much less is Self-enquiry an empty formula, for it involves an intense activity of the entire mind to keep it steadily poised in pure Self-awareness.

Self-enquiry is the one infallible means, the only direct one, to realise the unconditioned, Absolute Being that you really are.

D: Why should Self-enquiry alone be considered the direct means to *jnana*?

M: Because every kind of *sadhana* except that of *atma vichara* presupposes the retention of the mind as the instrument for carrying on the *sadhana*, and without the mind it cannot be practised. The ego may take different and subtler forms at the different stages of one's practice, but is itself never destroyed.

When Janaka exclaimed, "Now I have discovered the thief who has been ruining me all along. He shall be dealt with summarily", the King was really referring to the ego or the mind.

D: But the thief may well be apprehended by the other *sadhanas* as well.

M: The attempt to destroy the ego or the mind through *sadhanas* other than *atma vichara*, is just like the thief assuming the guise of a policeman to catch the thief, that is himself. *Atma vichara* alone can reveal the truth that neither the ego nor the mind really exists, and enables one to realise the pure, undifferentiated Being of the Self or the Absolute.

Having realised the Self, nothing remains to be known, because it is perfect Bliss, it is the All.

D: In this life beset with limitations can I ever realise the bliss of the Self?

M: That bliss of the Self is always with you, and you will find it for yourself, if you would seek it earnestly.

The cause of your misery is not in the life without; it is in you as the ego. You impose limitations on yourself and then make a vain struggle to transcend them. All unhappiness is due to the ego; with it comes all your trouble. What does it avail you to attribute to the happenings in life the cause of misery which is really within you? What happiness can you get from things extraneous to yourself? When you get it, how long will it last?

If you would deny the ego and scorch it by ignoring it, you would be free. If you accept it, it will impose limitations on you and throw you into a vain struggle to transcend them. That was how the thief sought to 'ruin' King Janaka.

To *be* the Self that you really are is the only means to realise the bliss that is ever yours.

D: Not having realised the truth that the Self alone exists, should I not adopt *bhakti* and *yoga margas* as being more suitable for purposes of *sadhana* than *vichara marga*? Is not the realization of one's Absolute Being that is, *Brahma jnana*, something quite unattainable to a layman like me?

M: *Brahma jnana* is not a knowledge to be acquired, so that acquiring it one may obtain happiness. It is one's ignorant outlook that one should give up. The Self you seek to know is verily yourself. Your supposed ignorance causes you needless grief like that of the ten foolish men who grieved the 'loss' of the tenth man who was never lost.

The ten foolish men in the parable forded a stream and on reaching the other shore wanted to make sure that all of them had in fact safely crossed the stream. One of the ten began to count, but while counting others, left himself out. "I see only nine; sure enough, we have lost one. Who can it be?" he said. "Did you count correctly?" asked another, and did the counting himself. But he too counted only nine. One after the other each of the ten counted only nine, missing himself. "We are only nine" they all agreed, "but who is the missing one?" they asked themselves. Every effort they made to discover the 'missing' individual failed. "Whoever he be that is drowned", said the most sentimental of ten fools, "we have lost him". So saying he burst into tears, and the rest of the nine followed suit.

Seeing them weeping on the river bank, a sympathetic wayfarer enquired for the cause. They related what had happened and said that even after counting themselves several times they could find no more than nine. On hearing the story, but seeing all the ten before him, the wayfarer guessed what had happened. In order to make them know for themselves that they were really ten, that all of them had come safe from the crossing, he told them "Let each of you count for himself but one after the other serially, one, two, three and so on, while I shall give you each a blow so that all of you may be sure of having been included in the count, and included only once. The tenth 'missing' man will then be found." Hearing this they rejoiced at the prospect of finding their 'lost' comrade and accepted the method suggested by the wayfarer.

While the kind wayfarer gave a blow to each of the ten in turn, he that got the blow counted himself aloud. "Ten" said the last man as he got the last blow in his turn. Bewildered they looked at one another, "We *are* ten" they said with one voice and thanked the wayfarer for having removed their grief.

That is the parable. From where was the tenth man brought in? Was he ever lost? By knowing that he had been there all the while, did they learn anything new? The cause of their grief was not the real loss of any one of the ten, it was their own ignorance, rather their mere supposition that one of them was lost (though they could not find who he was), because they had counted only nine.

Such is also the case with you. Truly there is no cause for you to be miserable and unhappy. You yourself impose limitations on your true nature of Infinite Being, and then weep that you are but a finite creature. Then you take up this or that *sadhana* to transcend the non-existent limitations. But if your *sadhana* itself assumes the existence of the limitations, how can it help you to transcend them?

Hence I say, know that you are really the Infinite, Pure Being, the Self Absolute. You are always that Self and nothing but that

Self. Therefore, you can never be really ignorant of the Self; your ignorance is merely a formal ignorance, like the ignorance of the ten fools about the 'lost' tenth man. It is this ignorance that caused them grief.

Know then that true knowledge does not create a new Being for you, it only removes your 'ignorant ignorance'. Bliss is not added to your nature, it is merely revealed as your true and natural state, eternal and imperishable. The only way to be rid of your grief is to know and be the Self. How can this be unattainable?

11

Sadhana and Grace

D: Research on God has been going on from time immemorial. Has the final word been said?

M: (Keeps Silence for some time).

D: (Puzzled) Should I consider Sri Bhagavan's silence as the reply to my question?

M: Yes. *Mauna* is *Iswara svarupa*. Hence the text:

मौनव्याख्या प्रकटितपरब्रह्मतत्त्वम् [1]

D: Buddha is said to have ignored such enquiries about God.

M: And, for this he was called a *sunya vadin* (nihilist). In fact Buddha concerned himself more with directing the seeker to realise Bliss here and now than with academic discussions about God etc.

D: God is described as manifest and unmanifest. As the former He is said to include the world as a part of His Being. If that is so, we as part of that world should have easily known Him in the manifested form.

M: Know yourself before you seek to decide about the nature of God and the world.

D: Does knowing myself imply knowing God?

M: Yes, God is within you.

D: Then, what stands in the way of my knowing myself or God?

M: Your wandering mind and perverted ways.

---

[1] The truth of Supreme Brahman proclaimed through silent eloquence.

D: I am a weak creature. But why does not the superior power of the Lord within remove the obstacles?

M: Yes, He will, if you have the aspiration.

D: Why should He not create the aspiration in me?

M: Then surrender yourself.

D: If I surrender myself, is no prayer to God necessary?

M: Surrender itself is a mighty prayer.

D: But is it not necessary to understand His nature before one surrenders oneself?

M: If you believe that God will do for you all the things you want Him to do, then surrender yourself to Him. Otherwise let God alone and know yourself.

D: Has God or the Guru any solicitude for me?

M: If you seek either — they are not really two but one and identical — rest assured that they are seeking you with a solicitude greater than you can ever imagine.

D: Jesus gave the parable of the lost coin, wherein the woman searches for it till it is found.

M: Yes, that aptly represents the truth that God or the Guru is always in search of the earnest seeker. Were the coin a dud piece, the woman would not have made that long search. Do you see what it means? The seeker must qualify himself through devotion etc.

D: But one may not be quite sure of God's Grace.

M: If the unripe mind does not feel His Grace, it does not mean that God's Grace is absent, for it would imply that God is at times not gracious, that is, ceases to be God.

D: Is that the same as the saying of Christ, "According to thy faith be it done unto thee".

M: Quite so.

D: The *Upanishads* say, I am told, that he alone knows the Atman whom the Atman chooses. Why should the Atman choose at all? If it chooses, why some particular person?

M: When the sun rises, some buds alone blossom, not all. Do you blame the sun for that? Nor can the bud blossom of itself, it requires the sunlight to do it.

D: May we not say that the help of the Atman is needed because it is the Atman that drew over itself the veil of *maya*?

M: You may say so.

D: If the Atman has drawn the veil over itself, should it not itself remove the veil?

M: It will do so. See for whom is the veil.

D: Why should I? Let the Atman itself remove the veil!

M: If the Atman talks about the veil, then the Atman itself will remove it.

D: Is God personal?

M: Yes, He is always the first person, the I, ever standing before you. Because you give precedence to worldly things, God appears to have receded to the background. If you give up all else and seek Him alone He alone will remain as the I, the Self.

D: The final state of Realization according to *Advaita*, is said to be the absolute Union with the Divine and according to *Visishtadvaita*, a qualified union, while *Dvaita* maintains that there is no union at all. Which of these should be considered the correct view?

M: Why speculate as to what will happen some time in the future? All are agreed that the 'I' exists. To whichever school of thought he may belong, let the earnest seeker first find out what the 'I' is. Then it will be time enough to know what the final State will be, whether the 'I' will get merged in the Supreme Being or stand apart from Him. Let us not forestall the conclusion, but keep an open mind.

D: But will not some understanding of the final state be a helpful guide even to the aspirant?

M: No purpose is served in trying to decide now what the final state of Realization will be. It has no intrinsic value.

D: Why so?

M: Because you proceed on a wrong principle. Your ascertainment has to depend on the intellect which shines only by the light it derives from the Self. Is it not presumptuous on the part of the intellect to sit in judgement over that of which it is but a limited manifestation, and from which it derives its little light?

How can the intellect which can never reach the Self be competent to ascertain, and much less decide the nature of the final state of Realization? It is like trying to measure the sunlight at its source by the standard of the light given by a candle. The wax will melt down before the candle comes anywhere near the sun.

Instead of indulging in mere speculation, devote yourself here and now to the search for the Truth that is ever within you.

111

The Jnani and the World

D: Is the world perceived by the *jnani*?

M: From whom is the question? Is it from a *jnani* or *ajnani*?

D: From an *ajnani*, I admit.

M: Is it the world that seeks to decide the issue about its reality? The doubt arises in you. Know in the first instance who the doubter is, and then you may consider if the world is real or not.

D: The *ajnani* sees and knows the world and its objects, which affect his senses of touch, taste etc. Does the *jnani* experience the world in like manner?

M: You talk of seeing and knowing the world. But without knowing yourself, the knowing subject, (without whom there is no knowledge of the object), how can you know the true nature of the world, the known object? No doubt, the objects affect the body and the sense organs, but is it to your body that the question arises? Does the body say "I feel the object, it is real"? Or is it the world that says to you "I, the world, am real"?

D: I am only trying to understand the *jnani's* point of view about the world. Is the world perceived after Self-realization?

M: Why worry yourself about the world and what happens to it after Self-realization? First realise the Self. What does it matter if the world is perceived or not. Do you gain anything to help you in your quest by the non-perception of the world during sleep? Conversely, what would you lose now by the perception of the world? It is quite immaterial to the *jnani* or *ajnani* if he perceives the world or not. It is seen by both, but their viewpoints differ.

D: If the *jnani* and the *ajnani* perceive the world in like manner, where is the difference between them?

M: Seeing the world, the *jnani* sees the Self which is the substratum of all that is seen; the *ajnani*, whether he sees the world or not, is ignorant of his true Being, the Self.

Take the instance of moving pictures on the screen in the cinema-show. What is there in front of you before the play begins? Merely the screen. On that screen you see the entire show, and for all appearances the pictures are real. But go and try to take hold of them. What do you take hold of? Merely the screen on which the pictures appeared so real. After the play, when the pictures disappear, what remains? The screen again!

So with the Self. That alone exists; the pictures come and go. If you hold on to the Self, you will not be deceived by the appearance of the pictures. Nor does it matter at all if the pictures appear or disappear. Ignoring the Self the *ajnani* thinks the world is real, just as ignoring the screen he sees merely the pictures, as if they existed apart from it. If one knows that without the seer there is nothing to be seen, just as there are no pictures without the screen, one is not deluded. The *jnani* knows that the screen, the pictures and the sight thereof are but the Self. With the pictures the Self is in its manifest form; without the pictures It remains in the unmanifest form. To the *jnani* it is quite immaterial if the Self is in the one form or the other. He is always the Self. But the *ajnani* seeing the *jnani* active gets confounded.

D: It is just that point that prompted me to put my first question, whether one who has realised the Self perceives the world as we do, and if he does, I should like to know how Sri Bhagavan felt about the mysterious disappearance of the photo yesterday....

M: (Smiling) You are referring to the photo of the Madurai temple. A few minutes earlier it was passing through the hands of the visitors who looked at it in turn. Evidently, it was mislaid among the pages of some book or other they were consulting.

D: Yes, it was that incident. How does Bhagavan view it? There was anxious search for the photo which, in the end, could not be found. How does Bhagavan view the mysterious disappearance of the photo, just at the moment when it was wanted?

M: Suppose you dream that you are taking me to your distant country, Poland. You wake up and ask me, "I dreamt so and so. Did you also have some such dream or know in some other way that I was taking you to Poland?" What significance will you attach to such an enquiry?

D: But, with regard to the missing photo, the whole incident took place in front of Sri Bhagavan.

M: The seeing of the photo, its disappearance as well as your present enquiry are all mere workings of mind.

There is a *Puranic* story which illustrates the point. When Sita was missing from the forest hermitage, Rama went about in search of her, wailing, 'O Sita, Sita!' It is said that Parvati and Parameswara saw from above what was taking place in the forest. Parvati expressed her surprise to Siva and said "You praised Rama as the Perfect Being. See how he behaves and grieves at the loss of Sita!" Siva replied "If you are sceptical about Rama's perfection, then put him to the test yourself. Through your *yoga maya* transform yourself into the likeness of Sita and appear before him". Parvati did so. She appeared before Rama in the very likeness of Sita, but to her astonishment Rama ignored her presence and went on as before, calling out 'O Sita, O Sita!', as if he were blind.

D: I am unable to grasp the moral of the story.

M: If Rama were really searching for the bodily presence of Sita, he would have recognised the person who was standing in front of himself as the Sita he had lost. But no, the missing Sita was just as unreal as the Sita that appeared before his eyes. Rama was not really blind; but to Rama, the *jnani*, the prior being of Sita in the hermitage, her disappearance, his consequent search for her as well as the actual presence of Parvati in the guise of

Sita, were all equally unreal. Do you now understand how the missing photo was viewed?

D: I cannot say it is all clear to me. Is the world that is seen, felt and sensed by us in so many ways something like a dream, an illusion?

M: There is no alternative for you but to accept the world as unreal, if you are seeking the Truth and the Truth alone.

D: Why so?

M: For the simple reason that unless you give up the idea that the world is real, your mind will always be after it. If you take the appearance to be real you will never know the Real itself, although it is the Real alone that exists. This point is illustrated by the analogy of the 'snake in the rope'. As long as you see the snake you cannot see the rope as such. The non-existent snake becomes real to you, while the real rope seems wholly non-existent as such.

D: It is easy to accept tentatively that the world is not ultimately real, but it is hard to have the conviction that it is really unreal.

M: Even so is your dream world real while you are dreaming. So long as the dream lasts, everything you see, feel, etc., therein is real.

D: Is then the world nothing better than a dream?

M: What is wrong with the sense of reality you have while you are dreaming? You may be dreaming of something quite impossible, for instance, of having a happy chat with a dead person. Just for a moment you may doubt in the dream saying to yourself, 'Was he not dead?', but somehow your mind reconciles itself to the dream vision, and the person is as good as alive for the purposes of the dream. In other words, the dream as a dream does not permit you to doubt its reality. Even so, you are unable to doubt the reality of the world of your wakeful experience. How can the mind which has itself created the world accept it as unreal? That is the significance of the comparison made between the world of wakeful experience and the dream world.

Both are but creations of the mind and so long as the mind is engrossed in either, it finds itself unable to deny the reality of the dream world while dreaming and of the waking world while awake. If, on the contrary, you withdraw your mind completely from the world and turn it within and abide thus, that is, if you keep awake always to the Self, which is the substratum of all experience, you will find the world, of which alone you are now aware, just as unreal as the world in which you lived in your dream.

D: As I said before, we see, feel and sense the world in so many ways. These sensations are the reactions to the objects seen, felt etc., and are not mental creations as in dreams, which differ not only from person to person but also with regard to the same person. Is that not enough to prove the objective reality of the world?

M: All this talk about inconsistencies and their attribution to the dream world arises only now, when you are awake. While you are dreaming, the dream was a perfectly integrated whole. That is to say, if you felt thirsty in a dream, the illusory drinking of illusory water did quench your illusory thirst. But all this was real and not illusory to you so long as you did not know that the dream itself was illusory. Similarly with the waking world; and the sensations you now have, get coordinated to give you the impression that the world is real.

If, on the contrary, the world is a self-existent reality (that is what you evidently mean by its objectivity) what prevents the world from revealing itself to you in sleep? You do not say you have not existed in your sleep.

D: Neither do I deny the world's existence while I am asleep. It has been existing all the while. If during my sleep I did not see it, others who are not sleeping saw it.

M: To say you existed while asleep, was it necessary to call in the evidence of others so as to prove it to you? Why do you seek their evidence now? Those 'others' can tell you of having seen the world (during your sleep) only when you yourself are awake.

With regard to your own existence it is different. On waking up you say you had a sound sleep, so that, to that extent you are aware of yourself in the deepest sleep, whereas you have not the slightest notion of the world's existence then. Even now, while you are awake, is it the world that says "I am real", or is it you?

D: Of course *I* say it, but I say it of the world.

M: Well then, that world, which you say is real, is really mocking at you for seeking to prove its reality while of your own Reality you are ignorant.

You want somehow or other to maintain that the world is real. What is the standard of Reality? That alone is Real which exists by itself, which reveals itself by itself and which is eternal and unchanging.

Does the world exist by itself? Was it ever seen without the aid of the mind? In sleep there is neither mind nor world. When awake there is the mind and there is the world. What does this invariable concomitance mean? You are familiar with the principles of inductive logic, which are considered the very basis of scientific investigation. Why do you not decide this question of the reality of the world in the light of those accepted principles of logic?

Of yourself you can say 'I exist'. That is, yours is not mere existence, it is Existence of which you are conscious. Really, it is Existence identical with Consciousness.

D: The world may not be conscious of itself, yet it exists.

M: Consciousness is always Self-consciousness. If you are conscious of anything you are essentially conscious of yourself. Unselfconscious existence is a contradiction in terms. It is no existence at all. It is merely attributed existence, whereas true Existence, the *sat*, is not an attribute, it is the Substance itself. It is the *vastu*. Reality is therefore known as *sat-chit*, Being-Consciousness, and never merely the one to the exclusion of the other. The world neither exists by itself, nor is it conscious of its existence. How can you say that such a world is real?

And what is the nature of the world? It is perpetual change, a continuous, interminable flux. A dependent, unselfconscious, ever-changing world cannot be real.

D: Not only does Western empirical science* consider the world real, but, the *Vedas* etc., give elaborate cosmological descriptions of the world and its origin. Why should they do so if the world is unreal?

M: The essential purpose of the *Vedas* etc., is to teach you the nature of the imperishable Atman, and to declare with authority "Thou art That".

D: I accept. But why should they give cosmological descriptions spun out at great length, unless they consider the world real?

M: Adopt in practice what you accept in theory, and leave the rest. The *sastras* have to guide every type of seeker after Truth, and all are not of the same mental make-up. What you cannot accept treat as *artha vada* or auxiliary argument.

* NOTE

In the last analysis, the world of sense-perception resolves itself into the two categories of time and space, and here is what Sir James Jeans writes in his book, *The New Background of Science*, as the conclusion drawn from experiments based on Einstein's Theory of Relativity.

"We find that space means nothing apart from our perception of objects, and time means nothing apart from our experience of events. Space begins to appear merely as *a fiction created by our own minds* (our physical bodies are merely things in space — *see* verse 16, *Truth Revealed*), an illegitimate extension to Nature of a subjective concept which helps us to understand and describe the arrangement of objects as seen by us; while time appears as a second fiction (without the past and the future, time as generally conceived is but a myth — *see* verse 15, *Truth Revealed*), serving a similar purpose for the arrangement of events which happen to us".

The reader should note that when time and space, are considered by modern science as mere fictions created by our own minds, objects and events become *ipso facto* mere creations of the mind (*see* verses 17 & 18 *Truth Revealed*) because they cannot be without time and space.

As to the solidity attributed by the layman to matter, the following conclusions drawn from modern experimental physics furnish the answer.

1. Science knows nothing about the real nature of the constituents of the atom. It knows only the radiations that come out of it, *but never the source itself.*

2. Since the atom continually radiates energy, the electron at one time can never be identified with the electron at another time.

3. 'The electron ceases altogether to have the properties of a "thing" as conceived by common sense; it is merely a *region* from which energy may radiate'. (*Outline of Philosophy* by Bertrand Russell).

The following is the conclusion Bertrand Russell draws: "Now owing chiefly to two German physicists, Heisenburg and Schrodinger, the last vestiges of the old solid atom have melted away, matter has become as ghostly as anything in a spiritualist *seance*".

Let the reader now judge for himself in what way the waking world of sense-perception is fundamentally different from the dream-world, reminding himself of what has been stated above in the body of the chapter and of the following from '*Who Am I?*': "Except that the wakeful state is long and the dream state is short, there is no difference between the two". This truth, echoed by modern science, is expressed by Dr. Eddington thus: "The frank realization that physical science is concerned with the world of shadows is one of the most significant advances.... *In the world of physics we watch a shadow-graph performance of the drama of familiar life* (the picture show on the screen, as Sri Bhagavan calls it). The shadow of my elbow rests on the shadow table as the shadow ink flows over shadow paper". (*The Nature of the Physical World*).

IV

The Heart is the Self

D: Sri Bhagavan speaks of the heart as the seat of Consciousness and as identical with the Self. What does the heart exactly signify?

M: The question about the heart arises because you are interested in seeking the source of consciousness. To all deep thinking minds, the enquiry about the 'I' and its nature has an irresistible fascination.

Call it by any name, God, Self, the heart or the seat of Consciousness, it is all the same. The point to be grasped is this, that Heart means the very core of one's being, the Centre, without which there is nothing whatever.

D: But Sri Bhagavan has specified a particular place for the heart within the physical body, that it is in the chest, two digits to the right from the median.

M: Yes, that is the centre of spiritual experience according to the testimony of Sages. This spiritual heart-centre is quite different from the blood-propelling, muscular organ known by the same name. The spiritual heart-centre is not an organ of the body. All that you can say of the heart is that it is the very core of your being. That with which you are really identical (as the word in Sanskrit literally means), whether you are awake, asleep or dreaming, whether you are engaged in work or immersed in *samadhi*.

D: In that case, how can it be localized in any part of the body? Fixing a place for the heart would imply setting physiological limitations to That which is beyond space and time.

M: That is right. But the person who puts the question about the position of the heart, considers himself as existing with or in the body. While putting the question now, would you say that your body alone is here but that you are speaking from somewhere else? No, you accept your bodily existence. It is from this point of view that any reference to a physical body comes to be made.

Truly speaking, Pure Consciousness is indivisible, it is without parts. It has no form and shape, no 'within' and 'without'. There is no 'right' or 'left' for it. Pure Consciousness, which is the heart, includes all; and nothing is outside or apart from it. That is the ultimate Truth.

From this absolute standpoint, the heart, Self or Consciousness can have no particular place assigned to it in the physical body. What is the reason? The body is itself a mere projection of the mind, and the mind is but a poor reflection of the radiant heart. How can That, in which everything is contained, be itself confined as a tiny part within the physical body which is but an infinitesimal, phenomenal manifestation of the one Reality?

But people do not understand this. They cannot help thinking in terms of the physical body and the world. For instance, you say, "I have come to this ashram all the way from my country beyond the Himalayas". But that is not the truth. Where is a 'coming' or 'going' or any movement whatever, for the one, all-pervading Spirit which you really are? *You* are where you have always been. It is your body that moved or was conveyed from place to place till *it* reached this ashram.

This is the simple truth, but to a person who considers himself a subject living in an objective world, it appears as something altogether visionary!

It is by coming down to the level of ordinary understanding that a place is assigned to the heart in the physical body.

D: How then shall I understand Sri Bhagavan's statement that the *experience* of the heart-centre is at the particular place in the chest?

M: Once you accept that from the true and absolute standpoint, the heart as Pure Consciousness is beyond space and time, it will be easy for you to understand the rest in its correct perspective.

D: It is only on that basis that I have put the question about the position of the heart. I am asking about Sri Bhagavan's experience.

M: Pure Consciousness wholly unrelated to the physical body and transcending the mind is a matter of direct experience. Sages know their bodiless, eternal Existence just as the layman knows his bodily existence. But the experience of Consciousness can be with bodily awareness as well as without it. In the bodiless experience of Pure Consciousness the Sage is beyond time and space, and no question about the position of the heart can then at all arise.

Since, however, the physical body cannot subsist (with life) apart from Consciousness, bodily awareness has to be sustained by Pure Consciousness. The former, by its nature, is limited to and can never be co-extensive with the latter which is infinite and eternal. Body-consciousness is merely a monad-like, miniature reflection of the Pure Consciousness with which the Sage has realised his identity. For him, therefore, body-consciousness is only a reflected ray, as it were, of the Self-effulgent, Infinite Consciousness which is himself. It is in this sense alone that the Sage is aware of his bodily existence.

Since, during the bodiless experience of the heart as Pure Consciousness, the Sage is not at all aware of the body, that absolute experience is localized by him within the limits of the physical body by a sort of feeling-recollection made while he is with bodily awareness.

D: For men like me, who have neither the direct experience of the heart nor the consequent recollection, the matter seems to be somewhat difficult to grasp. About the position of the heart itself, perhaps, we must depend on some sort of guesswork.

M: If the determination of the position of the heart is to depend on guesswork even in the case of the layman, the question is surely not worth much consideration. No, it is not on guesswork that you have to depend, it is on an unerring intuition.

D: For whom is the intuition?

M: For one and all.

D: Does Sri Bhagavan credit me with an intuitive knowledge of the heart?

M: No, not of the heart, but of the position of the heart in relation to your identity.

D: Sri Bhagavan says that I intuitively know the position of the heart in the physical body?

M: Why not ?

D: (Pointing to himself) It is to *me* personally — that Sri Bhagavan is referring?

M: Yes. That is the intuition! How did you refer to yourself by gesture just now? Did you not put your finger on the right side of the chest? That is exactly the place of the heart-centre.

D: So then, in the absence of direct knowledge of the heart-centre, I have to depend on this intuition?

M: What is wrong with it? When a schoolboy says "It is I that did the sum correctly", or when he asks you, "Shall I run and get the book for you", would he point out to the head that did the sum correctly, or to the legs that will carry him swiftly to get you the book? No, in both cases, his finger is pointed quite naturally towards the right side of the chest, thus giving innocent expression to the profound truth that the source of 'I'-ness in him is there. It is an *unerring* intuition that makes him refer to himself, to the heart which is the Self, in that way. The act is quite *involuntary* and *universal*, that is to say, it is the same in the case of every individual.

What stronger proof than this do you require about the position of the heart-centre in the physical body?

V

The Place of the Heart

D: But I have heard it said by a Saint that his spiritual experience is felt at the place between the eyebrows.

M: As I said previously, that is the ultimate and perfect Realization which transcends subject-object relation. When that is achieved, it does not matter where the spiritual experience is felt.

D: But the question is, which is the correct view of the two, namely, (1) that the centre of spiritual experience is the place between the eyebrows, (2) that it is the heart.

M: For purposes of practice you may concentrate between the eyebrows, it would then be *bhavana* or imaginative contemplation of the mind; whereas the supreme state of *anubhava* or Realization, with which you become wholly identified and in which your individuality is completely dissolved, transcends the mind. Then, there can be no objectified centre to be experienced by you as a subject distinct and separate from it.

D: I would like to put my question in slightly different words. Can the place between the eyebrows be said to be the seat of the Self?

M: You accept that the Self is the ultimate source of consciousness and that it subsists equally during all the three states of the mind. But see what happens when a person in meditation is overcome by sleep. As the first symptom of sleep his head begins to nod, which however cannot happen if the Self were situate between the eyebrows or at any other place in the head.

If during sleep the experience of the Self is not felt between the eyebrows, that centre cannot be called its seat without implying that the Self often forsakes its own place, which is absurd.

The fact is the *sadhaka* may have his experience at any centre or *chakra* on which he concentrates his mind. But, for that reason that particular place of his experience does not become *ipso facto* the seat of the Self.

There is an interesting story about Kamal, the son of Saint Kabir, which serves as an illustration to show that the head (and *a fortiori* the place between the eyebrows) cannot be considered the seat of the Self.

Kabir was intensely devoted to Sri Rama, and he never failed to feed those who sang the praise of the Lord of his devotion. On one occasion, however, it so happened that he had not the wherewithal to provide food for such a gathering of devotees. For him, however, there could be no alternative except that he must somehow make every necessary arrangement before next morning. So, he and his son set out at night to secure the required provisions.

The story goes that after the father and son had removed the provisions from a merchant's house through a hole they made in the wall, the son went in again just to wake up the household and tell them, as a matter of principle, that their house had been burgled. When, having roused the household, the boy tried to make good his escape through the hole and join his father on the other side, his body stuck up in the aperture. To avoid being identified by the pursuing household (because, if detected, there would be no feeding at all of the devotees the next day), he called out to his father and told him to sever his head and take it away with him. That done, Kabir made good his escape with the stolen provisions and the son's head which on reaching home, was hidden away from possible detection. The next day Kabir gave a feast to the *bhaktas*, quite unmindful of what had happened the previous night. "If it is Rama's will" said Kabir to himself, "that my son should die, may it prevail!" In the evening Kabir with the party set out as usual in procession into the town with *bhajana* etc.

Meanwhile, the burgled householder made report to the king, producing the truncated body of Kamal, which gave them no clue. In order to secure its identification, the king had the body tied up prominently on the highway so that whoever claimed or took it away (for, no dead body is forsaken without the last rites being given to it by the kith and kin) might be interrogated or arrested by the police who were posted secretly for the purpose.

Kabir and his party with the *bhajana* in full swing came by the highway, when, to the astonishment of all, Kamal's truncated body (which was considered dead as a door-nail) began to clap its hands marking time to the tune sung by the *bhajana* party.

This story disproves the suggestion that the head or the place between the eyebrows is the seat of the Self. It may also be noted that when in the battlefield the head of a soldier in action is severed from the body by a sudden and powerful stroke of the sword, the body continues to run or move its limbs as in a mock fight, just for a while, before it finally falls down dead.

D: But Kamal's body was dead hours before?

M: What you call death is really no extraordinary experience for Kamal. Here is the story of what had happened when he was younger still.

As a boy Kamal had a friend of equal age with whom he used to play games of marbles etc. A general rule they observed between themselves was that if one of them owed the other a game or two, the same should be redeemed the next day. One evening they parted with a game to the credit of Kamal. Next day, in order to claim 'the return of the game', Kamal went to the boy's house, where he saw the boy laid on the verandah, while his relatives were weeping beside him.

"What is the matter"? Kamal asked them, "he played with me last evening and also owes me a game". The relatives wept all the more saying that the boy was dead. "No", said Kamal, "he is not dead but merely pretends to be so, just to evade redeeming the game he owes me". The relatives protested, asking Kamal to see for himself that the boy was really dead, that the body was cold and stiff. "But all this is a mere pretension of the boy, I know; what if the body be stiff and cold? I too can become like that". So saying Kamal laid himself down, and in the twinkling of an eye was dead.

The poor relatives, who were weeping till then for the death of their own boy, were distressed and dismayed, and now began to weep for Kamal's death also. But up rose Kamal on his back, declaring "Do you see it now? I was as you would say dead, but I am up again, alive and kicking. This is how he wants to deceive me, but he cannot elude me like this with his pretensions".

In the end, the story goes, Kamal's inherent saintliness gave life to the dead boy, and Kamal got back the game that was due to him. The moral is that the death of the body is not the extinction of the Self. Its relation to the body is not limited by birth and death, and its place in the physical body is not circumscribed by one's experience felt at a particular place, as for instance between the eyebrows, due to practice of *dhyana* made on that centre. The supreme state of Self-awareness is never absent; it transcends the three states of the mind as well as life and death.

D: Since Sri Bhagavan says that the Self may function at any of the centres or *chakras* while its seat is in the heart, is it not possible that by the practice of intense concentration or *dhyana* between the eyebrows this centre may itself become the seat of the Self?

M: As long as it is merely the stage of practice of concentration by fixing a place of controlling your attention, any consideration about the seat of the Self would merely be a theorisation. You consider yourself as the subject, the seer, and the place whereon you fix your attention becomes the object seen. This is merely *bhavana*. When, on the contrary, you see the Seer himself, you merge in the Self, you become one with it; that is the heart.

D: Then, is the practice of concentration between the eyebrows advisable?

M: The final result of the practice of any kind of *dhyana* is that the object, on which the *sadhaka* fixes his mind, ceases to exist as distinct and separate from the subject. They (the subject and object) become the one Self, and that is the heart.

The practice of concentration on the centre between the eyebrows is one of the methods of *sadhana*, and thereby thoughts are effectively controlled for the time being. The reason is this. All thought is an extroverted activity of the mind; and thought, in the first instance, follows 'sight', physical or mental.

It should however be noted, that this *sadhana* of fixing one's attention between the eyebrows must be accompanied by *japa*. Because next in importance to *the physical eye* is *the physical ear*, either for controlling or distracting the mind. Next in importance to *the eye of the mind* (that is, mental visualisation of the object) is *the ear of the mind* (that is, mental articulation of speech), either to control and thereby strengthen the mind, or to distract and thereby dissipate it.

Therefore, while fixing the mind's eye on a centre, as for instance between the eyebrows, you should also practise the mental articulation of a *nama* (name) or *mantra* (sacred syllable or syllables). Otherwise you will soon lose your hold on the object of concentration.

Sadhana as described above leads to identification of the Name, Word or Self — whatever you may call it — with the centre selected for purposes of *dhyana*. Pure Consciousness, the Self or the heart is the final Realization.

D: Why does not Sri Bhagavan direct us to practise concentration on some particular centre of *chakra*?

M: *Yoga sastras* say that the *sahasrara* or the brain is the seat of the Self. *Purushasukta* declares that the heart is its seat. To enable the *sadhaka* to steer clear of possible doubt, I tell him to take up the 'thread' or the clue of 'I'-ness or 'I-am'-ness and follow it up its source. Because, firstly it is impossible for anybody to entertain any doubt about his 'I'-notion; secondly whatever be the *sadhana* adopted, the final goal is the realization of the source of 'I-am'-ness which is the primary datum of your experience.

If you, therefore, practise *atma vichara* you will reach the heart which is the Self.

VI

Aham and Aham-Vritti

D: How can any enquiry initiated by the ego reveal its own unreality?

M: The ego's phenomenal existence is transcended when you dive into the Source wherefrom arises the *aham-vritti*.

D: But is not the *aham-vritti* only one of the three forms in which the ego manifests itself? *Yoga Vasishtha* and other ancient texts describe the ego as having a threefold form.

M: It is so. The ego is described as having three bodies, the gross, the subtle and the causal, but that is only for the purposes of analytical exposition. If the method of enquiry were to depend on the ego's form, you may take it that any enquiry would become altogether impossible, because the forms the ego may assume are legion. Therefore, for purposes of *jnana vichara*, you have to proceed on the basis that the ego has but one form, namely that of *aham-vritti*.

D: But it may prove inadequate for realizing *jnana*.

M: Self-enquiry by following the clue of *aham-vritti* is just like the dog tracing its master by his scent. The master may be at some distant, unknown place, but that does not at all stand in the way of the dog tracing him. The master's scent is an infallible clue for the animal, and nothing else, such as the dress he wears, or his build and stature etc., counts. The dog holds on to that scent undistractedly while searching for him, and finally it succeeds in tracing him.

D: The question still remains why the quest for the source of *aham-vritti*, as distinguished from other *vrittis*, should be considered the direct means to Self-realization.

M: The word *'aham'* is itself very suggestive. The two letters of the word, namely A (*A*) and h (*HA*), are the first and the last letters of the Sanskrit alphabet. The suggestion intended to be conveyed by the word is that it comprises all. How? Because *aham* signifies existence itself.

Although the concept of 'I'-ness or 'I-am'-ness is by usage known as *aham-vritti*, it is not really a *vritti* like the other *vrittis* of the mind. Because, unlike the other *vrittis* which have no essential interrelation, the *aham-vritti* is equally and essentially related to each and every *vritti* of the mind. Without the *aham-vritti* there can be no other *vritti*, but the *aham-vritti* can subsist by itself without depending on any other *vritti* of the mind. The *aham-vritti* is therefore fundamentally different from other *vrittis*.

So then, the search for the source of the *aham-vritti* is not merely the search for the basis of one of the forms of the ego but for the very Source itself from which arises the 'I-am'-ness. In other words, the quest for and the realization of the source of the ego in the form of *aham-vritti* necessarily implies the transcendence of the ego in everyone of its possible forms.

D: Conceding that the *aham-vritti* essentially comprises all the forms of the ego, why should that *vritti* alone be chosen as the means for Self-enquiry?

M: Because it is the one irreducible datum of your experience; because seeking its source is the only practicable course you can adopt to realise the Self. The ego is said to have a causal body, but how can you make it the subject of your investigation? When the ego adopts that form, you are immersed in the darkness of sleep.

D: But is not the ego in its subtle and causal forms too intangible to be tackled through the enquiry into the source of *aham-vritti* conducted while the mind is awake?

M: No. The enquiry into the source of *aham-vritti* touches the very existence of the ego. Therefore the subtlety of the ego's form is not a material consideration.

D: While the one aim is to realise the unconditioned, pure Being of the Self, which is in no way dependent on the ego, how can enquiry pertaining to the ego in the form of *aham-vritti* be of any use?

M: From the functional point of view, the form, activity or whatever else you may call it (it is immaterial, since it is evanescent), the ego has one and only one characteristic. The ego functions as the knot between the Self which is Pure Consciousness and the physical body which is inert and insentient. The ego is therefore called the *chit-jada granthi*. In your investigation into the source of *aham-vritti*, you take the essential *chit* aspect of the ego; and for this reason the enquiry must lead to the realization of the pure consciousness of the Self.

D: What is the relation between the pure consciousness realised by the *jnani* and the 'I-am'-ness which is accepted as the primary datum of experience?

M: The undifferentiated consciousness of Pure Being is the heart or *hridayam* which you really are, as signified by the word itself (*hrit* + *ayam* = heart am I). From the heart arises the 'I-am'-ness as the primary datum of one's experience. By itself it is *suddha-sattva* in character. It is in this *suddha-sattva svarupa* (that is, uncontaminated by *rajas* and *tamas*), that the 'I' appears to subsist in the *jnani*........

D: In the *jnani* the ego subsists in the *sattvic* form and therefore it appears as something real. Am I right?

M: No. The existence of the ego in any form, either in the *jnani* or *ajnani* is itself an appearance. But to the *ajnani* who is deluded into thinking that the waking state and the world are real, the ego also appears to be real. Since he sees the *jnani* act like other individuals, he feels constrained to posit some notion of individuality with reference to the *jnani* also.

D: How then does the *aham-vritti* function in the *jnani*?

M: It does not function in him at all. The *jnani's lakshya* is the heart itself, because he is one and identical with that undifferentiated, Pure Consciousness referred to by the

Upanishads as the *Prajnana*. *Prajnana* is verily Brahman, the Absolute and there is no Brahman other than *Prajnana*.

D: How then does ignorance of this one and only Reality unhappily arise in the case of the *ajnani*?

M: The *ajnani* sees only the mind which is a mere reflection of the light of Pure Consciousness arising from the heart. Of the heart itself he is ignorant. Why? Because his mind is extroverted and has never sought its Source.

D: What prevents the infinite, undifferentiated light of Consciousness arising from the heart from revealing itself to the *ajnani*?

M: Just as water in the pot reflects the enormous sun within the narrow limits of the pot, even so the *vasanas* or latent tendencies of the mind of the individual, acting as the reflecting medium, catch the all-pervading, infinite light of Consciousness arising from the heart and present in the form of a reflection the phenomenon called the mind. Seeing only this reflection, the *ajnani* is deluded into the belief that he is a finite being, the *jiva*.

If the mind becomes introverted through enquiry into the source of *aham-vritti*, the *vasanas* become extinct, and in the absence of the reflecting medium the phenomenon of reflection, namely, the mind, also disappears being absorbed into the light of the one Reality, the heart.

This is the sum and substance of all that an aspirant needs to know. What is imperatively required of him is an earnest and one-pointed enquiry into the source of *aham-vritti*.

D: But any endeavour he may make is limited to the mind in the waking state. How can such enquiry conducted in only one of the three states of the mind destroy the mind itself?

M: Enquiry into the source of *aham-vritti* is, no doubt, initiated by the *sadhaka* in the waking state of the mind. It cannot be said that in him the mind has been destroyed. But the process of Self-enquiry will itself reveal that the alternation or transmutation of the three states of the mind, as well as the three states themselves, belong to the world of phenomena which cannot affect his intense, inward enquiry.

Self-enquiry is really possible only through intense introversion of the mind. What is finally realised as a result of such enquiry into the source of *aham-vritti*, is verily the heart as the undifferentiated light of Pure Consciousness, into which the reflected light of the mind is completely absorbed.

D: For the *jnani*, then, there is no distinction between the three states of mind?

M: How can there be, when the mind itself is dissolved and lost in the light of Consciousness?

For the *jnani* all the three states are equally unreal. But the *ajnani* is unable to comprehend this, because for him the standard of reality is the waking state, whereas for the *jnani* the standard of Reality is Reality itself. This Reality of Pure Consciousness is eternal by its nature and therefore subsists equally during what you call waking, dreaming and sleep. To him who is one with that Reality, there is neither the mind nor its three states, and therefore, neither introversion nor extroversion.

His is the ever-waking state, because he is awake to the eternal Self; his is the ever dreaming state, because to him the world is no better than a repeatedly presented phenomenon of dream; his is the ever-sleeping state, because he is at all times without the 'body-am-I' consciousness.

D: Should I then consider Sri Bhagavan as talking to me in a waking-dreaming-sleeping state?

M: Because your conscious experience is now limited to the duration of the extroversion of the mind, you call the present moment the waking state, whereas all the while your mind has been asleep to the Self, and therefore you are now really fast asleep.

D: To me sleep is a mere blankness.

M: That is so, because your waking state is a mere effervescence of the restless mind.

D: What I mean by blankness is that I am hardly aware of anything in my sleep; it is for me the same as non-existence.

M: But you did exist during sleep.

D: If I did, I was not aware of it.

M: You do not mean to say in all seriousness you ceased to exist during your sleep! (Laughing). If you went to sleep as Mr. X, did you get up from it as Mr. Y?

D: I know my identity, perhaps, by an act of memory.

M: Granting that, how is it possible unless there is a continuity of awareness?

D: But I was unaware of that awareness.

M: No. Who says you are unaware in sleep? It is your mind. But there was no mind in your sleep? Of what value is the testimony of the mind about your existence or experience during sleep? Seeking the testimony of the mind to disprove your existence or awareness during sleep is just like calling your son's evidence to disprove your birth!

Do you remember, I told you once previously that existence and awareness are not two different things but one and the same? Well, if for any reason you feel constrained to admit the fact that you existed in sleep be sure you were also aware of that existence.

What you were really unaware of in sleep is your bodily existence. You are confounding this bodily awareness with the true Awareness of the Self which is eternal. *Prajnana*, which is the source of 'I-am'-ness, ever subsists unaffected by the three transitory states of the mind, thus enabling you to retain your identity unimpaired.

Prajnana is also beyond the three states, because it can subsist without them and in spite of them.

It is that Reality that you should seek during your so called waking state by tracing the *aham-vritti* to its Source. Intense practice in this enquiry will reveal that the mind and its three states are unreal and that you are the eternal, infinite consciousness of Pure Being, the Self or the Heart.

APPENDIX

Bhagavan Sri Ramana Maharshi

By Sri Swami Siddeshwarananda

Sri Swami Siddheswarananda was an erudite scholar of the Vedanta *and a distinguished member of the* Order of Sri Ramakrishna Mission, *and was in charge of its branch at Paris.*

While in India, he was a frequent visitor of the ashram, and was an ardent devotee of Bhagavan Sri Ramana Maharshi whom he adored as the living incarnation of the Truth, one with the universe as a whole, the Self of All.

This article is condensed from the English translation done by Major A. W. Chadwick, O. B. E., of the original article in French

SRI RAMANA MAHARSHI EXPOUNDS A SYSTEM OF thought and philosophy of life, which incarnates the essence of *Vedantic* teachings. In India a philosophy of life can have absolutely no influence except when it is reflected in the life of the one who expounds it. We ought also to say that it is the life of an individual and his 'realizations' which give opportunity for the construction of a philosophical system, and such a life brings an understanding and opens a horizon which affects society as a whole and improves the relationship amongst men.

When the prophets of ancient India attained the ultimate truths which they expressed forthwith in *Vedic* hymns and the teachings of the *Upanishads*, they were looked upon as the salt of the earth, because they became lighthouses which guide hesitating humanity on its path. The truths which these great beings discovered are hidden in their soul. And what they teach man is only the means of penetrating into himself to bring forth into the day the secret treasure which all possess. It is the aspect of the right of each one to make his own introspection which confers dignity on man's efforts, because Truth is our legitimate inheritance.

The *Upanishads* address themselves in these terms to all those who aspire after the Truth: "O, ye inheritors of immortal bliss!" Can anything more encouraging exist than these words of hope? It is not in the original sin that man finds the basis of his existence, it is in the golden flame of the light of Atman.

The Maharshi has discovered this; he found it of his own accord, without any exterior help. A very young scholar, he was overtaken by a fear of death. He threw away books, which veil more often than they reveal the Truth; he extended himself on the ground, closed his eyes and imitated all the symptoms of death.

The following is what he himself has said about this experience:

> Now death has come, what does it mean? What is it that has died? The material body dies. I at once dramatized the scene of death. I extended my limbs and held them rigid. I held my breath. 'Very well,' I told myself, 'this body is dead, they will come and take it to the cremation ground and reduce it to ashes. But when the body is dead, am I dead? This body, is it I? It is inert, and moreover I feel my personality independent of it. I am then the deathless Spirit transcending the body which alone lives and dies'. All this rose before me intensely, without having to be expressed, as living truth perceived immediately and almost without argument. The fear of death disappeared entirely and definitely. This conscious and immediate presence of the 'I' or Self altogether independent of the physical body, has continued ever since.

This direct experience of the Self is called *Aparokshanubhuti*; it is distinct from all knowledge obtained by intellectual effort which always implies a relation between the subject and object, and consequently is limited by space and time, and is without any transcendental value.

He who has had this direct experience of the Self is considered to be Liberated even while he is still alive. He is called a *Jivanmukta*. The existence of such individuals who are living incarnations of the Truth, renders this Truth demonstrable. The *Vedantic* realization of these great beings gives in effect the possibility of a practical application, and their realizations raise the level of human consciousness.

It is this aspect of *Vedanta* which has attracted towards its teachings the attention of savants. *Vedantic* research goes much deeper than all objective analysis of matter, it goes to the fundamental basis of perception and as such gives us a synopsis of the Truth rather than a curtailed view. The interest that the West takes in the life and teachings of Sri Ramana Maharshi proves the universal attraction of *Vedanta*, which one can see embodied in the Sage of Tiruvannamalai.

In an article on Indian Yoga, M. Lacombe of the Paris University has written about the Maharshi:

> His person sheds a force consisting of intelligence and mastery of the Self. A flashing eye, intense and fixed without hardness, Olympian softness of gesture, slender and delicate in an immobile body, he is considered by excellent judges to be a very authentic *Yogi* and to have reached the highest Realization.

I cite this passage only to show the impression produced by a visit to Maharshi on one who appreciates the atmosphere that surrounds the Sage.

It is, however, very difficult for an European, moulded in the traditions of Theology and Western Philosophy, to have any contact whatsoever with the conception of Maharshi's life.

I would respectfully observe to the learned professor that the Maharshi is much rather a *tattva jnani* than a *yogi*; his conception of life embraces all life, which for an Indian embraces the three states, *jagrat, svapna* and *sushupti*. The *yogic* is the experience of 'I' as cosmic identification which takes the *jagrat* as the essential field of experience. If one would find examples of this cosmic and universal experience of the 'I', as M. Lacombe calls it, there is no lack of mystics in India who have reached sufficient realization on this basis of experience.

But the Maharshi is above all a *tattva jnani* and the field of his search and experience is much greater than that of a mystic. The Sage transcends the limits of the three states.

The Maharshi accepts the terminology sanctioned by tradition and always employed by the sages of India since the time of the *Upanishads*.

The teachings of Maharshi are in perfect accord with the philosophical and spiritual scriptures of ancient India and proceed directly from the great Sages of the past.

Whoever has occasion to examine at first hand the Maharshi, knows full well that he is neither an 'extrovert' nor an 'introvert'. He is the most normal man that one could ever find. He is in effect a *sthitaprajna*, a man whose intelligence is solidly founded. I have seen him apparently plunged in himself, when everybody believed him to be absorbed in his own Self, but when at this moment someone at the end of the hall made a mistake in the recitation of certain Tamil verses, the Maharshi opened his eyes, corrected the mistake, then again closed his eyes and returned to his former state. I have already stated that one cannot say that the exterior world does not interest him. He has reached an extraordinary degree of concentration, and as that concentration perpetually rests on an habitual state of life in *jnana* or — as the Sage calls it — *sahajasthiti*, he is neither an introvert nor an extrovert. Just simply, he IS. And by his knowledge of the ultimate Reality he is one with That in its expression of multiplicity of manifestation, he is one with the Universe as a whole.

When I saw him I found in him the perfect example of the description which Sri Sankaracharya gives in his *Vivekachudamani*, when he explains what characterises a *Jivanmukta*. Verse 429 reads:

लीनधीरपि जागर्ति जाग्रद्धर्मविवर्जितः ।
बोधो निर्वासनो यस्य स जीवन्मुक्त इष्यते ॥

"He who even when his mind is merged in Brahman, is nevertheless entirely awake, but is at the same time free from the characteristics of the waking state, and whose realization is free from all desire, should be considered a man liberated while still alive".

The notion of introversion and extroversion cannot be applied to one whose philosophy of life reposes uniquely on the experience of the waking state.

In the *Panchadasi*, which is an authoritative work on *Advaita*, we find in Verse 13 of Chapter VI, a statement which is extremely important on this point. The author, Vidyaranya, says:

नाप्रतीतिस्तयोर्बाधः किन्तु मिथ्यात्वनिश्चयः ।
नो चेत्सुषुप्तिमूर्च्छादौ मुच्येतायत्नतो जनः ॥

"The destruction of the world and of the *jiva* does not signify that they should become imperceptible to the senses, but there should arise a determination of their unreal nature. If such is not the case, people may find emancipation without making any personal effort, as in dreamless sleep or in a swoon (when all perceptions disappear completely)".

As the *Gita* says, the Atman, forgetting its real nature, believes that it is the ego and the author of all actions, which is the cause of all misunderstanding. A man like the Maharshi, who has transcended the ego, is considered by the *Upanishads* to be the Self of All.

If we could but spend sometime by the side of the Maharshi, we should then be able to understand better in the light of words spoken by the Sage on philosophical problems that life of illumination, like the great fire which burns on the Hill Arunachala, is a veritable lighthouse for those who wish to find in modern India the revivifying effects of the teachings of the *Upanishads* consecrated by time.

GLOSSARY

(The numbers in brackets after each word indicate the pages on which that word is used)

A

Abhyasa: spiritual practice. (24)

Advaita: non-duality; also the doctrine of non-dualism. (16, 43, 71)

Aham: 'I'. (62)

A ham-vritti: the 'I-thought', the limited feeling of 'I-ness'. (62-67)

Ajnana: ignorance of one's own true nature. (19)

Ajnani: a person who is ignorant of his true nature. (19, 20, 45, 46, 64-66)

Anubhava: experience, especially the experience of Self-knowledge. (57)

Aparokshanubhuti: direct experience (of Self-knowledge). (69)

Artha-Vada: explanatory argument given to suit a particular purpose. (51)

Asan: posture, especially a posture adopted for meditation. (3)

Asramam: the abode of a Sage or ascetic. (13)

Atman: the real Self. (42, 43, 50, 69)

Atma-jnani: a person who has attained Self-knowledge. (16)

Atma-vichara: Self-enquiry, the practice of scrutinizing or attending to the feeling 'I' in order to find out 'Who am I?' (38, 61)

Atma-vidya: Self-knowledge. (25)

B

Bhajana: singing of devotional songs. (30, 59)

Bhakta: devotee. (59)

Bhakti: devotion. (17, 39)

Bhavana: imagination, meditation. (57, 60)

Brahma-jnana: knowledge of *Brahman.* (39)

Brahman: the absolute, non-dual reality, which is the Self or *Atman.* (64, 71)

C

Chakra: one of the six main yogic centres in the body. (60, 61)

Chidananda: the bliss of pure consciousness. (9)

Chit: pure consciousness, which is the nature of the real Self. (64)

Chit-jada-granthi: the knot between the Self, which is pure consciousness, and the body, which is insentient. (64)

D

Dehatma-buddhi: the feeling 'I am this body'. (20)

Dhyana: meditation. (17, 18)

Dvaita: duality; also the doctrine of dualism. (16, 43)

G

Gita: the *Bhagavad Gita*, one of the most renowned Hindu scriptures. (6, 17, 72)

Guru: a true spiritual teacher, who is one with God or the real Self. (26-29, 42)

Guru-kripa: the Grace of the Guru. (26)

Grihasta: a householder, a person leading a married life. (4)

H

Hridayam: the Heart, which is the real Self. (64)

I

Iswara-svarupa: the nature of God or Iswara. (41)

J

Jada: insentient. (6)

Jagrat: the waking state. (20, 70)

Jagrat-sushupti: the state of wakeful sleep, in which there are no thoughts but in which there is full awareness of the existence-consciousness 'I am'. (6, 20)

Japa: repetition of a *mantra* or a name of God. (18, 31, 61)

Jiva: an individual soul. (6, 7, 19, 65)

Jivanmukta: a person who is liberated even while living in the body. (21, 69, 71)

Jnana: knowledge, especially knowledge of the real Self. (17, 18, 24, 36, 38, 62, 71)

Jnana-vichara: Self-enquiry, enquiry leading to *Jnana* or Self-knowledge. (62)

Jnani: a person who has attained Self-knowledge. (7, 20, 21, 45-47, 64, 66)

K

Karma-yogi: a person whose actions are not motivated by desire for personal benefit or by any other kind of attachment. (16)

Kevala nirvikalpa samadhi: a temporary state of *samadhi* or Self-absorption. (8, 9)

L

Lakshya: target (on which attention is focussed), that which is kept in view. (21, 64)

M

Maharshi: a great Sage. (68-72)

Mantra: a sacred formula used for *japa* or repetition. (37, 61)

Marga: a spiritual path. (39)

Maya: delusion. (42)

Moksha: liberation. (4, 29)

Mauna: silence. (10, 41)

N

Nama: a name (of God). (61)

Nama-japa: repetition of a name of God. (18)

Namaskar: the act of obeisance. (3)

Nirvana: the state of liberation or egolessness. (21)

Nirvikalpa samadhi: the state of Self-absorption. (8, 9, 21)

P

Prarabdha: destiny, the portion of the fruit of one's past actions which are allotted to be experienced in this lifetime. (3, 20, 21)

Prasad: food offered to the Guru or a deity, a portion of which may be returned to the devotee as a sign of blessing. (28)

Purusha Sukta: a hymn from the Rig Veda. (61)

Prajnana: pure consciousness. (64, 67)

R

Rajas: the second of the three *gunas* or qualities of nature, namely the quality of restlessness, desire and passion. (64)

Rishi: a Sage. (29)

S

Sadhana: a spiritual practice, a means adopted for spiritual progress. (38-40, 41, 60, 61)

Sadhaka: a person who practises *sadhana.* (57, 60)

Sahaja jnani: a person who abides in his natural state, having attained Self-knowledge. (9)

Sahaja nirvikalpa samadhi: the permanent and natural state of *samadhi* or complete Self -absorption. (8, 9)

Sahaja-sthiti: the natural state. (71)

Sahasrara: the brain, described metaphorically as a thousand-petalled lotus. (61)

Samadhi: the state of Self-absorption, in which (as defined by Sri Bhagavan on p. 23) "there is only the feeling I am' and no thoughts". (4, 6-9, 20, 23, 24, 31, 53)

Samsara: the state of mundane activity or worldly existence. (15)

Samskara: a mental impression or tendency continuing from former lives. (19)

Sannyasa: renunciation. (4)

Sannyasin: a renunciate. (4, 10)

Sastras: the scriptures. (51)

Sat: true existence or being. (50)

Sat-chit: existence-consciousness. (50)

Sattva: the first of the three *gunas* or qualities of nature, namely the quality of calmness, goodness and purity. (64)

Sattvic: of the nature of *Sattva.* (64)

Siddhis: occult powers. (24)

Sri Bhagavata: one of the eighteen *puranas,* a sacred text centred mainly around the life of Sri Krishna. (17)

Sthita-prajna: a person who firmly abides in the state of Self-knowledge. (71)

Suddha-sattva: uncontaminated purity or *sattva.* (64)

Suddha-sattva svarupa: the form of uncontaminated *sattva.* (64)

Sunya-vadin: an atheist, a person who denies the existence of God or any ultimate reality. (41)

Sushupti: dreamless sleep. (20, 70)

Svapna: dream. (20, 70)

T

Tamas: the last of the three *gunas* or qualities of nature, namely the quality of darkness ignorance and evil. (64)

Tattva-jnani: a person who knows the reality. (70)

Truth Revealed: the work *Ulladu Narpadu* by Bhagavan Sri Ramana. (51)

U

Upanishads: the later and more philosophical portions of the Vedas. (68-70, 72)

V

Vairagya: desirelessness. (18)

Vasana: a mental tendency continuing from former lives. (22, 65)

Vasana-kshaya: the destruction of all *vasanas.* (22)

Vastu: the reality or ultimate substance. (50)

Vedas: the oldest of the Hindu scriptures. (50)

Vedanta: the philosophy of the *Upanishads.* (15, 68-70)

Vichara: enquiry or scrutiny, that is, the practice Self-enquiry or *atma vichara.* (18, 31)

Vichara marga: the path of Self-enquiry. (39)

Visishtadvaita: the doctrine of qualified non-dualism (43)

Vritti: thought, activity of the mind. (62, 63)

W

Who am I?: the work *Nan Yar?* by Bhagavan Ramana. (52)

Y

Yoga: literally 'union' or 'uniting'; this word is used in many different senses, but generally denotes the path of *raja yoga* expounded by the Sage Patanjali. (15)

Yoga marga: the path of *raja yoga.* (39)

Yoga-maya: the power to veil the nature of something and to create an illusory appearance. (47)

Yoga-sastras: the scriptures which expound the path of *raja yoga.* (61)

Yoga-Vasishtha: a renowned sacred text which expounds the path of knowledge or *jnana yoga.* (62)

Yogi: an adept in *yoga*. (29, 70)

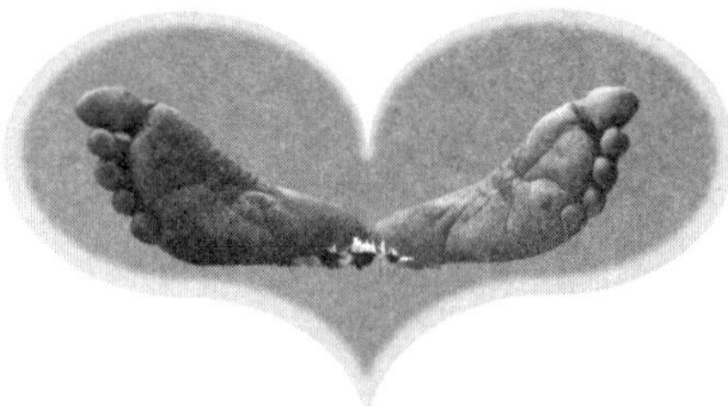

OM TAT SAT

SRI RAMANARPANAMASTU